DECORATING WITH
TRADITIONAL FABRICS

Miranda Innes

DECORATING WITH TRADITIONAL FABRICS

Simply made soft furnishings for today's home

Reader's Digest

THE READER'S DIGEST ASSOCIATION, INC.
Pleasantville, New York/Montreal

A READER'S DIGEST BOOK

Conceived, edited, and designed by Collins & Brown Limited

The acknowledgments that appear on page 128 are
hereby made part of this copyright page

Editor: **Colin Ziegler**
Art Director: **Roger Bristow**
Designer: **Steven Wooster**
Photographer: **Clive Streeter**
Stylist: **Lucinda Egerton**

Library of Congress Cataloging in Publication Data

Innes, Miranda
    Decorating with traditional fabrics : simply made soft furnishings
for today's home / Miranda Innes.
        p.   cm.
    Includes index.
    ISBN 0-89577-611-1
    1. Household linens. 2. Machine sewing. 3. Textile fabrics in
interior decoration. I. Title.
TT387.I55 1995
646.2'1—dc20   94-26967

Printed in Italy

Contents

BEDDING

SEATING

CURTAINS

TABLECLOTHS AND BAGS

Introduction

FABRIC IS ONE of the most important features for home decoration. With the glorious range of fabrics available, you can easily transform the look of any room in the house – whether by making a new duvet cover for your bedroom, curtains for your living room, pillows to complement your sofa, or a tablecloth for your dining table. You can recreate styles and designs found in different regions of the world or adapt them to suit your surroundings and personal preferences. Fabric offers an infinite variety of colors, patterns, and textures to choose from, giving you the chance to display your individuality, and create a special ambience in your home with the minimum cost and effort.

Walk into any good textile store and a new world of color, texture, and pattern opens up. There are undyed fabrics – cotton, linen, silk, and wool – and fabrics colored by natural dyes – indigo and madder, logwood and onion skins – in soft shades that look good in any setting. There are kaleidoscopes of color: purple, turquoise, chrome yellow, and magenta that wake up the senses. There are spots and stripes in all sizes and color combinations: understated, delicate sprig prints; richly patterned damasks and brocades; transparent voiles. You no longer need rely on the whims of manufacturers and whatever patterns and color schemes happen to be in vogue.

By mixing and matching colors, patterns, and textures you can give your home personality and individuality. Try varying the color scheme from one room to another: perhaps warm, inviting shades of pinks and russets for a cozy sitting room; sober, crisp stripes for a library or study; bright, light colors for a sunny breakfast room; cool greens for a sunroom. Think about how you can use fabrics to enhance your home. The curtains you choose can transform the whole mood of a room – you might try delicate muslin curtains for an airy, casual feel, or heavy brocade for a more formal setting. You can easily disguise an unattractive side table with a colorful table-cloth or transform a battered old sofa with a luxurious woolen throw.

In a world where people travel regularly to exotic locations, you need not restrict yourself to one decorative style. Guatemalan curtains are as welcome in a New York penthouse as in a *hacienda*; the classic, colorful designs of Shaker quilts turn up all over the world; simple, French café curtains have universal appeal. If you find a particular piece of fabric attractive, use it.

The items shown in this book are all made from traditional fabrics that have an enduring, universal appeal: dainty but boldly colored Provençal cotton; crisp, striped ticking; calico and lace; denim and tweed. These are fabrics that have stood the test of time and will look just as good in decades to come.

But if the fabrics are traditional, the items made from them have been designed with contemporary lifestyles in mind. This is a book for today's homemakers, for those who recoil from the formality of conventional soft furnishings but want to create a stylish living environment as quickly as possible with minimum effort. Each item can be made in a matter of hours and all the techniques are clearly explained so that you can pick up basic sewing skills as you go.

But this book is only a starting point for your own creative endeavors. It gives you a taste of the materials and colors that are available to you, and a hint of how they can be successfully and stylishly combined to produce a whole range of furnishings. You may choose to re-create the items exactly as demonstrated here. You may like the style of a particular item but feel that the color scheme or pattern would look out of place in your own home. You can look at the variations we suggest, or branch out on your own, choosing the fabric color and pattern yourself and following the instructions given here for making up the items. Using fabrics is an art, not an unchanging science. There are no hard-and-fast rules. You may not get it right every time, but with experience you will gain an intuitive feel for what works and what does not.

Techniques

Measuring Up

With each project, we give precise measurements for how much fabric you need to buy. However, your final requirements will naturally vary according to personal needs. In this section, we give instructions for calculating how much fabric you need to make bedding, curtains, pillows, and tablecloths for your home.

Shrinkage Before buying furnishing fabric, it is important to check for shrinkage. Ask a store assistant whether your chosen fabric will shrink during laundering and, if necessary, buy additional fabric to allow for this – sometimes it is necessary to buy as much as one-third extra to allow for shrinkage. Always machine wash your fabric and lining to preshrink them before cutting and making up, just in case they shrink at different rates.

Colorfastness When buying furnishing fabric you should also check for colorfastness. This is especially important if you are combining different fabrics in one project – for example, if you are making a patchwork quilt. If possible, avoid buying non-colorfast fabrics. If you do decide to buy them, however, remember to dry clean your item to prevent the colors from running.

Piecing If what you are making involves piecing – such as with the Flying Geese Quilt or the Patchwork Wool Pillow – you must remember to allow extra fabric for all the seam allowances of the different pieces of fabric. As a general rule allow ⅜in (1cm) on the edges of each piece of fabric to be sewn together (see also specific projects).

BEDDING

Flat Sheets To estimate the length of fabric needed for a flat sheet, first measure from the head of the mattress to the foot of the mattress. Next, measure the mattress depth. The length

of the sheet should equal the length plus twice the depth, plus 20in (50cm) tucking-under allowance, and 5in (12cm) for top and bottom hems. The width of fabric is calculated similarly. First measure from one side of the mattress to the other. Next, measure the mattress depth. The width of the sheet should equal the width plus twice the depth, plus 20in (50cm) tucking-under allowance, and 1½in (4cm) for hem allowances. For example, if you had a bed with a mattress 80in (203cm) long, 72in (183cm) wide, and 8in (20cm) deep, you would need a piece of fabric 121in (305cm) × 109½in (277cm).

Duvet Covers Duvets come in a variety of different sizes such as full size, 80 × 88in (200 × 220cm), and twin, 68 × 88in (170 × 220cm). For a duvet cover, you will need two pieces of fabric, each the length of your duvet plus ⅜in (1cm) for each seam allowance and 1⅜in (3.5cm) for the hems; and the width of your duvet plus ⅜in (1cm) for each side seam allowance. If the duvet cover has a facing, you will need another strip of fabric the width of your duvet, 4in (10cm) deep, plus ⅜in (1cm) for each seam allowance.

Quilts To estimate fabric for a quilt or coverlet, make up the bed with whatever will go under the quilt – like pillows and duvets – to arrive at the quilt's final dimensions. First, measure from the top of the bed down to the end, and add 10in (25cm) for the overhang and ⅜in (1cm) for each seam allowance. Next, measure the width of the bed and add 20in (50cm) for the overhang (10in [25cm] on either side) and ⅜in (1cm) for each seam allowance. 10in (25cm) gives a generous overhang, but you can vary this to your taste and to how high the bed is from the floor.

Pillowcases To calculate the fabric required for a plain pillowcase, start by measuring the length and width of your pillow. You will need a piece of fabric twice the pillow length plus 8in

(20cm) for flap and seam allowances, and once the pillow width plus ⅜in (1cm) for each seam allowance.

CURTAINS AND SHADES

Curtains The amount of fabric required for curtains depends on the window treatment you choose. Before measuring, it is important that you install all hardware – for example, tracks, rods, and runners – since the curtains should be made to fit the supporting device, not the window.

To calculate the finished length of your curtain (or curtains), measure from the top of the rod or track to the place where the hem will fall, either floor length or sill length. If you are making floor-length curtains, subtract ⅜in (1cm) from this measurement to allow the curtains to clear the floor. Next, add hem and heading allowances. Your heading allowance will vary according to the type of heading you choose (refer to manufacturer's instructions for individual requirements). Average hem allowances are 2in (5cm) for lightweight curtains and 3–6in (7.5–15cm) for heavier curtains, depending on their weight.

When estimating the finished width of your curtains, it is generally better to be generous rather than too exact. First measure the length of your rod or track, then multiply this measurement to give adequate fullness. If you are working with sheer or lightweight fabrics, multiply by three; for heavyweight fabrics, two, or, exceptionally, as little as one and a half times the finished width should suffice. To this width, add seam allowances (see each project for measurements), then divide the total by the width of your fabric. This will give the number of panels required.

Finally, to estimate the total length of fabric required, multiply the length of each curtain (including hem and heading allowances) by the total number of panels needed.

Lining will give your curtains a professional finish and will also help to keep out sunlight which might cause fading. When estimating lining requirements, always buy the same quantities as your chosen curtain material. If possible, buy lining fabric in the same width as your curtain fabric so seams match.

Cupboard Curtains These can be flat, gathered, or pleated, and your fabric requirements will depend on the style you choose and on the way the curtains are fitted. For fastening curtains with an elasticated rod, measure the length of the opening and add 5in (12.5cm) for seam allowances and channels for rods. Measure the width of the opening and multiply by two to three for gathered curtains and by three for pleated curtains. Add on 1in (2.5cm) for each side hem.

Use an elasticated rod (above) to hang cupboard curtains. Attach it to the cupboard with hooks and eyelets.

Tie-backs To establish the finished length of a tie-back, draw the curtain back as desired and measure around with a measuring tape, adding ⅜in (1cm) for each seam allowance. The width of the tie-back will vary according to the weight of your fabric – for example, narrow tie-backs suit sheer curtains, while heavy curtains require something wider. A guideline is 3–5in (8–13cm). The width of fabric you require is twice the finished width plus ⅜in (1cm) for each seam.

For braided tie-backs (see p. 74), you need three strips of fabric, each 8in (20cm) wide, and the required length of your tie-back plus 6in (15cm) to allow for the shortening effect of the batting and braiding, and ⅜in (1cm) for each seam allowance.

Roller Shades To determine the amount of fabric needed for a roller shade, first measure the width of your window recess. Deduct 1¼in (3cm) from this measurement to prevent the shade from catching in the brackets and add 2in (5cm) for hems. To estimate the length of fabric required for roller shades, measure the drop from the top of the window recess to the window

sill. Add at least 1in (2.5cm) at the top to allow for securing the fabric to the roller, and 2 ¼in (5.75cm) at the bottom for hems (this can vary according to the width of your lath).

PILLOWS

These vary considerably in size and shape, but for the purposes of this book we have concentrated on the square and rectangular knife-edge variety. For a pillow made from a single piece of fabric, you will need a piece twice the pillow length plus ⅜in (1cm) for each seam allowance, and the width plus ⅜in (1cm) for each seam allowance. If the pillow you are making has a different front and back, you need two pieces of fabric, each the length plus ⅜in (1cm) for each seam allowance, and the width plus ⅜in (1cm) for each seam allowance. You will need additional fabric depending on the type of closing employed. See individual projects for details.

TABLECLOTHS

Begin by measuring the length of your table top, through the middle, then measure the width. Now measure from the edge of the table top to the bottom of the required overhang; add ⅜in (2cm) for hem allowances. The amount of fabric needed is the table length plus double the overhang, and hem allowances; and the table width plus double the overhang and hem allowances. If your tablecloth is for a dining table, the overhang should be at least 10in (25cm) clear of the ground. For example, if you had a table measuring 72in (183cm) × 36in (91cm), standing 30in (76cm) from the ground, you need a piece of fabric 112¾in (287cm) × 76¾in (195cm).

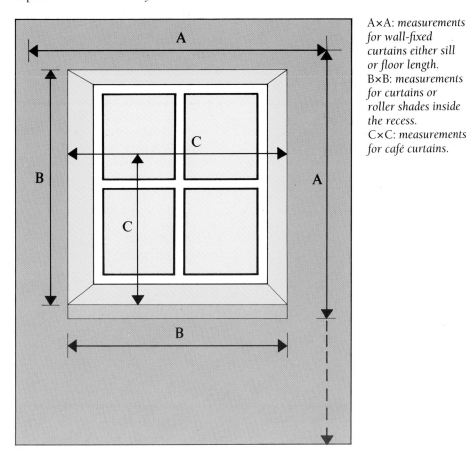

A×A: measurements for wall-fixed curtains either sill or floor length. B×B: measurements for curtains or roller shades inside the recess. C×C: measurements for café curtains.

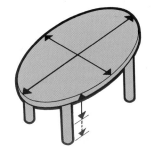

For occasional tables which are decorative rather than strictly functional, the table-cloth can be floor-length or even longer.

Preparing Your Cloth

Before you begin cutting, it is important to prepare your fabric carefully by straightening the ends of the cloth and pressing out creases. There are three methods of straightening the raw edges: tearing, drawing a thread, and cutting along a prominent pattern line, such as a stripe. While tearing is suitable for firmly woven fabrics, such as cotton shirting, it is unsuitable for knitted or loosely woven fabrics. To tear across the straight of grain, begin by snipping into one of the selvages using a pair of scissors. Next, grasp the fabric firmly with both hands and rip across to the opposite selvage to produce a straight edge. If your fabric is not suitable for tearing, you can draw out a thread and then cut along that line. First cut into the selvage, then gently pull the rip open to reveal the loose threads. Grasp one or two of the crosswise threads with your fingers and pull gently. The cloth will begin to gather up and, eventually, you will be able to pull out the entire thread. Now cut across the resulting straight line using a pair of scissors. Alternatively, let the pattern of the fabric be a guide for cutting.

Multiple Cutting If you are making something that requires a number of pieces of the same fabric all the same size, you can save time by cutting out several pieces at once. To do this, fold your fabric over and over until it is the maximum thickness you can cut through. Press the top layer of the fabric, making sure there are no wrinkles in the layers underneath, and pin all the layers together, checking that the edges line up. Mark the top layer of the fabric with the desired shape, pinning beside the marks to hold the fabric in place when cutting, and cut through all the layers at the same time. Be sure to fold and cut the fabric so that there is as little waste as possible. If the fabric you are using has a pattern or a stripe, be sure that the pattern or stripe is consistent on the different layers so that the cut pieces are all the same.

Cutting a Circle To cut a circle from a square piece of fabric, first fold the piece of fabric in half diagonally to form a triangle three times (see below). Press the fabric, making sure all the outer edges match up. Tie a piece of string around a tack and push the tack into the corner of the triangle that would be the center of the fabric if it were opened out (see bottom). Attach the other end of the piece of string to a pencil (as close to the point as possible) so that when the string is pulled taut, the distance from the tack to the pencil is the desired radius. With the pencil absolutely vertical, draw an arc. Pin the layers of fabric together outside this line and cut along it.

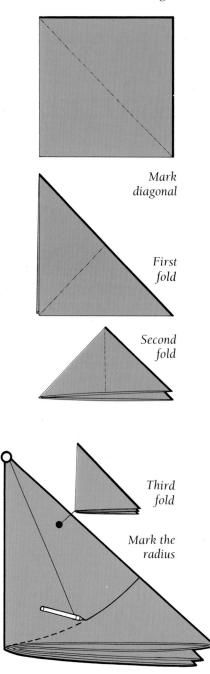

Mark diagonal

First fold

Second fold

Third fold

Mark the radius

Cutting a Circle

Basic Stitches

Basting Stitch Also known as a tacking stitch, this is a temporary stitch used to hold together several layers of fabric during making up as a more secure alternative to pinning. The basting stitch consists of a series of repeated straight stitches, each about ¼in (6mm) in length. You can baste with ordinary sewing thread, but it is best to use basting thread, which is weaker than ordinary thread and therefore easier to remove.

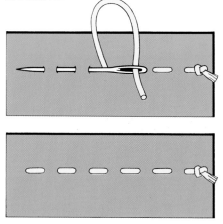

Basting Stitch

Blanket Stitch This is a decorative hand stitch which traditionally was used to finish the edges of thick woolen blankets, hence the name. Begin by turning under a hem on the wrong side. Next, secure the thread in the hem and insert the needle into the fabric from the right side about ⅜in (1cm) from the edge (**A**). Holding the working thread under the needle (**B**), pull through to create a loop. Repeat the process at ⅜in (1cm) intervals.

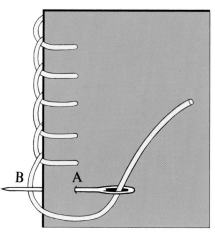

Blanket Stitch

Buttonhole Stitch Similar to the blanket stitch, the buttonhole stitch gives a firm, knotted edge that is ideal for neatening handworked buttonholes. With the edge of the fabric away from you, insert the needle upward through the fabric about ⅛in (3mm) from the raw edge. Twist the working thread around the tip of the needle, then pull the needle through to create a knot at the edge. Spacing can be large or small, depending on the purpose – for example, for hand buttonholes the stitches are made with no space in between. For machine-worked buttonholes, refer to your manufacturer's booklet.

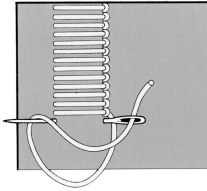

Buttonhole Stitch

Herringbone Stitch This stitch is ideal for hemming heavy fabrics, such as the door curtain on p. 70, because it enables you to neaten the raw edges as you sew. Stitches are worked from left to right, with the needle pointing left. First fasten the thread on the wrong side of the hem and bring the needle and thread through the hem edge (**A**). Take a very small stitch in the fabric directly above the hem edge and about ⅜in (1cm) to the right (**B**).

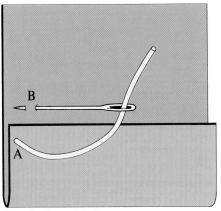

Herringbone Stitch

Take the next stitch ⅜in (1cm) to the right in the hem edge (**C**). Continue alternating stitches as illustrated.

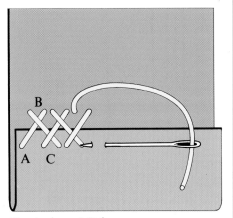

Herringbone Stitch

Slipstitch/Hemming Stitch This stitch is used when sewing a hem in place by hand. It is suitable for use on most fabrics and is ideal for use on lightweight fabrics. Working from right to left, fasten the thread and bring the needle out through the fold of the hem (**A**). Insert the needle into the main fabric and take a small stitch (**B**), taking care to catch only a few threads at a time so that the stitching will not show through on the right side. Opposite the first stitch, in the hem edge, insert the needle and slip it through the fold about ¼in (6mm) from the first stitch (**C**). Continue alternating as illustrated.

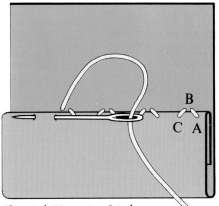

Slipstitch/Hemming Stitch

Stem Stitch This is a decorative stitch widely used for outlining letters and graphic images. Secure the thread on the wrong side and bring the needle through to the right side (**A**). Working from left to right, insert the needle back into the fabric (**B**) and bring it out

again half a stitch length between (**C**). Repeat the sequence, noting that C of the previous sequence becomes **A** in the next sequence.

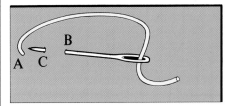

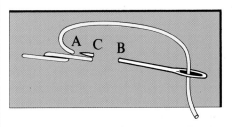

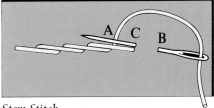

Stem Stitch

Reef Knot A reef knot (also called a square knot) is a secure method of tying cord. With a piece of cord in each hand, place the right cord (**A**) over the left (**B**) and bring the cord underneath (**1**). Now repeat the process, placing left cord over right (**2**). Pull tight (**3**).

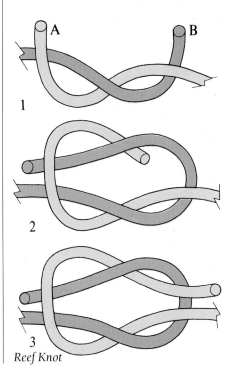

Reef Knot

Seams

Flat-fell Seam This is a sturdy seam ideal for items that need frequent laundering. It is used in making the Striped Pieced Curtains on the wrong side of the fabric, but can be used on the right side as a decorative feature. With right sides together (if used on the wrong side), pin and stitch along the seamline, making sure that one seam allowance is ¼in (6mm) bigger than the other (1). Press the seam to one side so that the wider seam allowance covers the narrower one (2). Turn the edge of the wider seam allowance under the narrower one and press. Stitch this folded edge in position, close to the edge (3).

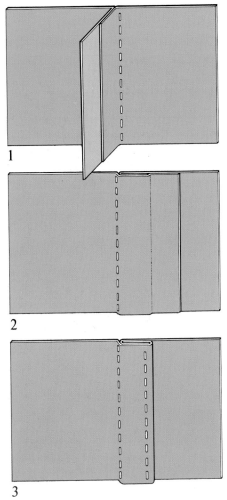

Flat-fell Seam

French Seam This seam is used mainly with lightweight fabrics to neaten and prevent fraying along straight edges. Pin the edges to be seamed wrong sides together and stitch ¼in (6mm) from raw edge (1). Turn,

press, and pin right sides together; stitch ⅜in (1cm) away from previous seam (2) and turn right side out.

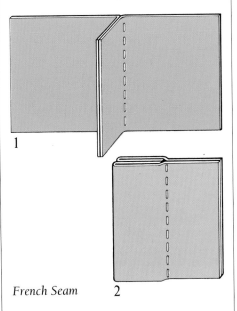

French Seam

Mitered Corners Corners can be neatly finished by mitering – the diagonal joining of two edges at a corner. First cut the border pieces to be joined at a 45° angle, leaving a ⅜in (1cm) seam allowance. Stitch the pieces together (see individual projects for whether right or wrong sides together), leaving ⅜in (1cm) unstitched at the inner ends (1). Pin and stitch the inner edges of the borders to the center panel all around (2) and press seams open. Trim the seams at the corners if they are too bulky.

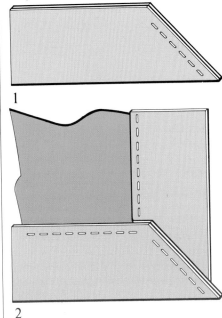

Mitered Corners

Mitered Binding To miter binding at corners, pin and stitch the first strip of binding to the edge of the fabric to be bound, right sides together and stopping ½in (1.25cm) from the corner (1). Pull the threads through and knot. Stitch the first strip of binding to the next strip in a right-angled "v" as shown, being careful not to stitch the main piece of fabric as well (2). Knot the thread ends. Cut the excess fabric to reduce bulk (2). Turn the second binding strip so that it lines up with the next edge of the main fabric and resume stitching, positioning the needle on the seam (3). Repeat to attach the other strips of binding. Turn all corners right side out and hem the back of the binding by hand (4).

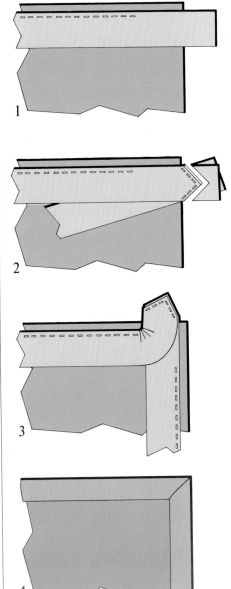

Mitered Binding

Stitching Corners For a neat, pointed corner, first stitch to the exact point at which you want your corner, leaving the needle in the fabric. Raise the presser foot and pivot the fabric 90°; replace the presser foot and continue stitching. When you have finished stitching, trim the seam allowance across the corner to reduce bulk as illustrated below.

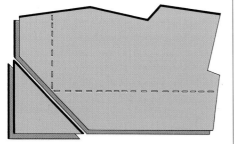

Stitching Corners

Stitching Binding at Corners Sew two strips of binding to opposite edges (1). Sew the other two strips onto the other edges so that they go on top of the first strips of binding at the corners. Tuck in the excess fabric at the ends (trim first if there is a lot of excess to reduce bulk) and stitch over the end to strengthen and neaten (2).

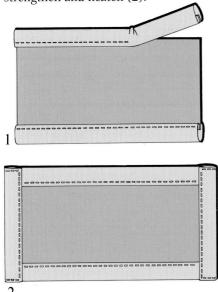

Stitching Binding at Corners

Stitching Curves A curved seam requires careful guidance as it passes under the needle so that the entire seamline ends up the same distance from the raw edge. In order to make the seam lie flat when turned right side out, you should clip into the curves with a pair of scissors after sewing, being careful not to cut the stitching itself. For curves that will be convex or outward when turned right side out, make small slits into the seam allowance (A). For curves that will be concave or inward when right side out, cut out small notches to reduce bulk (B).

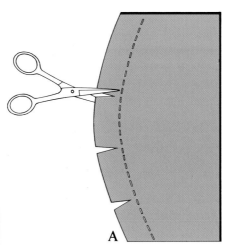

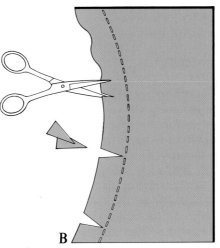

Stitching Curves

Basic Sewing Techniques

Choosing the Needle, Thread, and Stitch Length The type of needle, thread, and stitch length you should use depends upon the fabric you are stitching. For all of the projects in this book, you should use a regular, sharp-point needle. These come in a range of sizes from fine to coarse. As a general rule, use a finer needle for lightweight fabrics, a medium-sized needle for midweight fabrics, and a coarser needle for heavier fabrics. For all projects, normal sewing thread is suitable, but avoid polyester thread on fabrics where you will use a hot iron. The stitch length you select should vary according to the weight, texture, and structure of the fabric you are stitching. As a general rule, the heavier the fabric, the longer the stitch should be. Refer to the manufacturers' instructions for precise guidelines on using your machine.

Making Bias Binding Bias binding provides a neat and practical finish to many soft furnishings. It can be bought ready-made, but if it is not available in the fabric, color, or width that you require, you can make it yourself following the instructions given below.

Fold your fabric in half diagonally so that the straight edge on the crosswise grain is parallel to the lengthwise grain or selvage (1). Press the fabric across the diagonal fold and open out. Using the crease as a guide, mark parallel lines across the fabric, spacing them at the width required for your binding (2). Cut along the marked lines to produce bias strips.

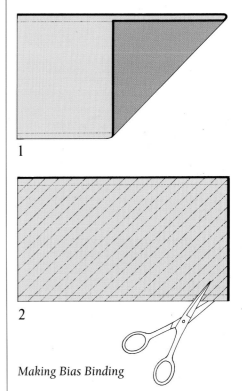

Making Bias Binding

To join bias strips together, trim the edges of each piece along the straight grain and mark ¼in (6mm) seam-lines. Pin the two strips right sides together, matching seamlines. Stitch and press seams open. Trim the protruding corners to align with the edge of the strip. If you are using patterned fabric, make sure the pattern matches up when joining the bias strips.

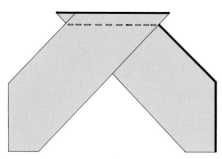

Joining Bias Strips

Making and Attaching Piping To make piping, wrap and pin a strip of bias binding around the piping cord, with wrong sides together, with ⅜in (1cm) seam allowance. Using a zipper foot and positioning the needle to the left of the foot, stitch close to the cord, taking care not to stitch into the piping cord.

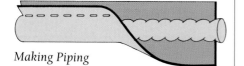

Making Piping

To attach piping, lay the piping on top of the right side of one of the pieces to be seamed so that the piping's seam allowance aligns with the edge of the fabric. Pin the other piece of fabric on top of the piping, right side facing the piping. Using a zipper foot, stitch along the seam just inside the piping stitches. At corners, cut notches out of the seam allowance to reduce bulk and make it lie flat.

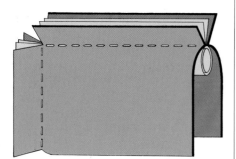

Attaching Piping

Making Pleats There are a number of different types of pleat. In this book (see the Cupboard Curtain and the Kilim Print Door Curtain) we use the knife pleat, where all the pleats lie in the same direction. To make knife pleats, pinch a fold of fabric to twice

the width you want the finished pleat to be, turn it over either to the right or left and pin and stitch it to the curtain. To calculate the amount of fabric the pleats will use up, allow twice the width of the pleat extra for every pleat there is. For example, if you want 10 pleats, each 2in (5cm) wide, you should allow an extra 40in (100cm) of fabric width for the pleats. If, as with the Cupboard Curtain, you want the pleats to go the whole way across the window or door, you need three times the width for the pleated area.

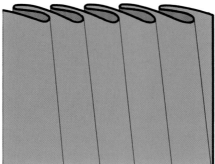

Making Pleats

Fastenings

Buttons When attaching buttons it is important to make sure that they are not attached too tightly. You can prevent this by stitching your button over a matchstick or toothpick. Begin by taking a few stitches at the mark where you want your button. Center the button over the mark, place the stick over the button, and sew the button in position through the holes. After a few stitches from back to front, slide the stick free. Lift the button away from the fabric so that the stitches are pulled taut. Finish by winding the thread firmly around the stitches under the button to create a shank. Knot neatly on the wrong side.

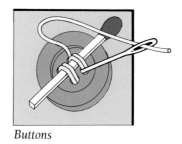

Buttons

Ties Ties make attractive fastenings for duvet covers and pillows. To make them, fold 1¼–2in (3–5cm) wide bias

strips (wider for duvet covers and narrower for pillows) in half lengthwise, wrong sides together, and turn under the raw edges at the sides and at the ends. Stitch together along the long edge and ends and press.

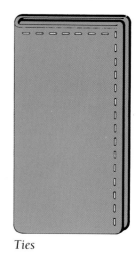

Ties

Zippers You can insert zippers across the back of a pillow cover or in one of its seams. First measure and mark the exact length of the opening, using your zipper as a guide. At both ends, stitch the seam right sides together, with a ½in (1.25cm) seam allowance, up to the opening. Press open a ½in (1.25cm) seam allowance for the zipper and pin the zipper in place on top of it, making sure the zipper pull is facing the outside (downward) and the tape is flat. Turn the pillow over and, using a zipper foot, stitch through all three layers – pillow cover, seam allowance, and zipper tape – down both sides of the zipper. Finish by pulling the threads through to the wrong side and tying in a reef knot. When stitching the pillow back to the front, leave the zipper partially open so that you can turn the pillow cover right side out.

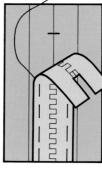
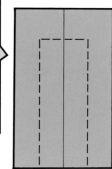

Zippers

Templates

Flying Geese Pillow and Quilt

The two templates on the left are for the Flying Geese Pillow (see p. 94) and the two on the right are for the Flying Geese Quilt (see pp. 36–41). All the templates allow for a ⅜in (1cm) seam all around and the dotted lines are the stitching lines. To make the templates, transfer the triangles onto cardboard with tracing paper and then cut them out.

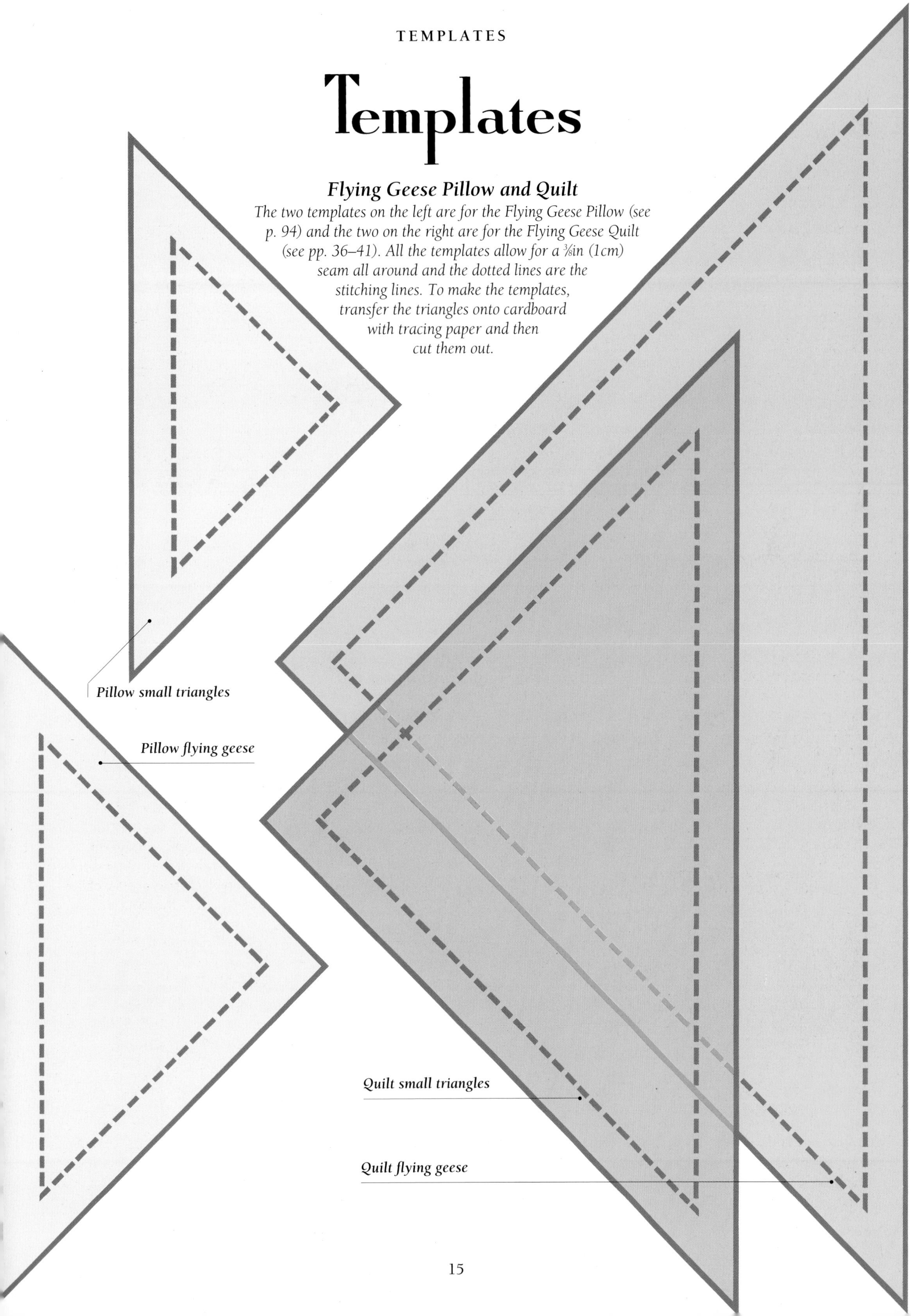

Pillow small triangles

Pillow flying geese

Quilt small triangles

Quilt flying geese

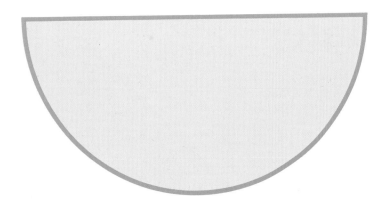

Café Curtain

*The template on the left is for the
decorative scallops (semicircles) at the top
of the Café Curtain (see pp. 60–63). To
make the template, transfer the semicircle
onto cardboard with tracing paper and cut
it out. You can shrink or enlarge the
semicircle to fit the size of your curtain or
the pattern of the fabric by using
a photocopier.*

Tartan Baby Quilt

*The templates below are for the hearts on the squares and at the
corners of the Tartan Baby Quilt (see pp. 46–51). To make the
templates, transfer the hearts onto cardboard with tracing paper
and cut them out. The smaller template for the corner hearts
allows for a ¼in (6mm) seam all around and the dotted line is the
stitching line. You can use the alphabet opposite if you want to
appliqué your child's initials onto the quilt instead of the hearts.
You can shrink or enlarge the letters to fit the size of the squares
on the quilt by using a photocopier.*

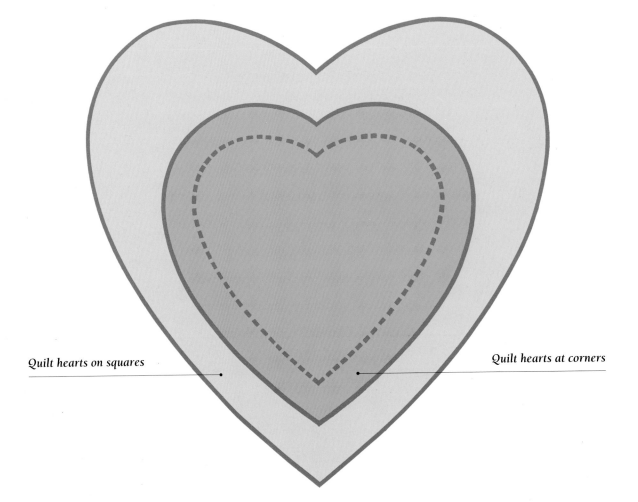

Quilt hearts on squares   *Quilt hearts at corners*

Embroidered Good Morning Pillow

The alphabet template (below) and the bluebird and morning glory design (below and opposite) are for the Embroidered Good Morning Pillow (see p. 94). Use dressmaker's carbon paper to transfer the design and whatever message you want directly onto the front cover of the pillow. Complete the stitching in stem stitch (see p. 11), using an embroiderer's frame to keep your work flat.

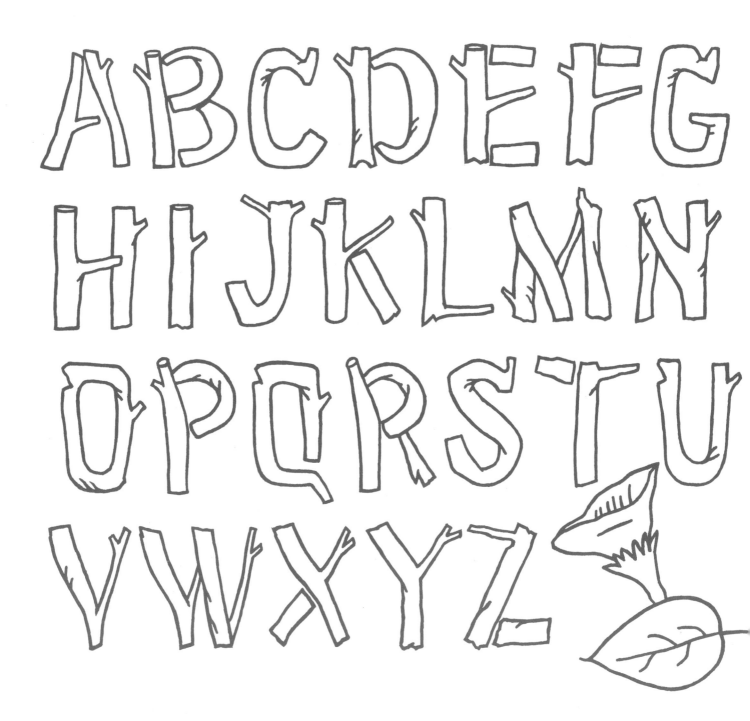

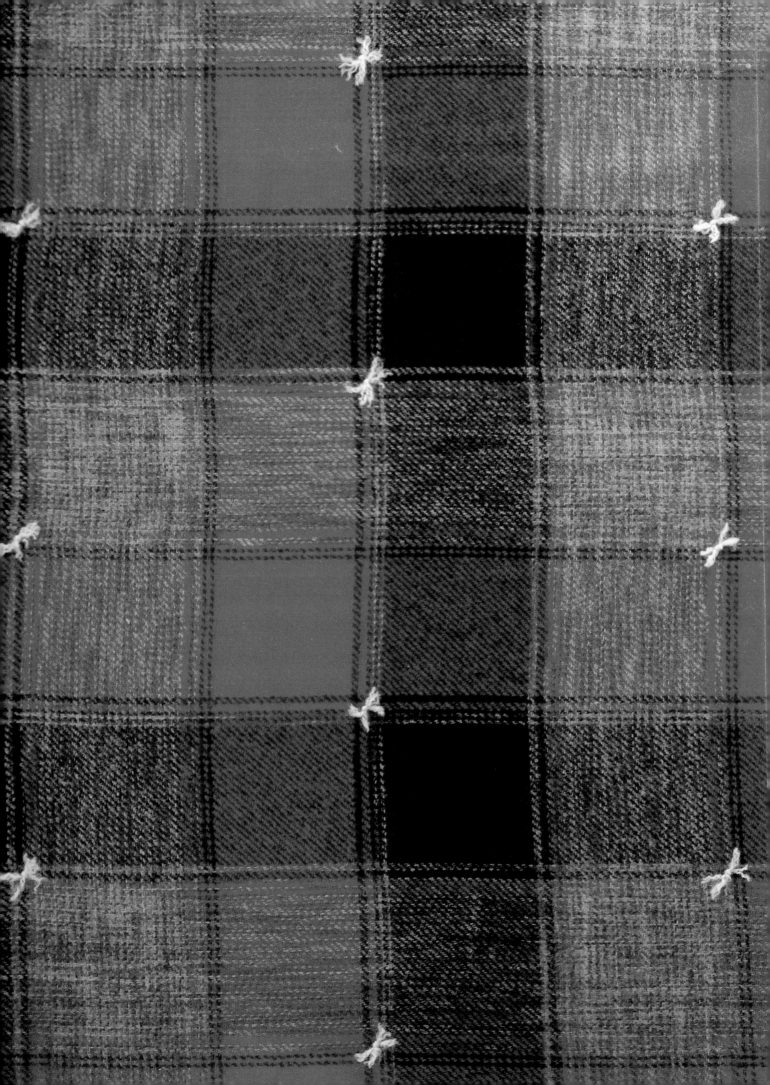

BEDDING

Striped Duvet Cover

An understated classic – a simple duvet cover in the style of a traditional coverlet from northern England, without the elaborate quilting.

THE APPEAL OF THIS duvet cover lies in its simplicity. It is inspired by a quilt called the "Durham Strippy", which was traditionally made in the north of England in the nineteenth century.

As here, the topside of these quilts consisted of nine strips of fabric all the same width but in alternating colors. Bold colors were often used for the strips – red and white being a favorite combination – and sometimes they were even pieced together from scraps. The quilts were filled with wool and backed with a single width of fabric, usually of a different color. The layers were secured together with elaborate quilting stitches which formed decorative motifs.

We have chosen fresh, cool colors to translate the strippy into a modern duvet cover. The wide stripes in the duvet top fit in particularly well with the design of the brass bed, and the sharp black binding further reinforces the visual link between the two. We have also introduced decorative ties as a means of closure, using the same fabric as the underside for the bottom ties and the same fabric as the duvet top's darker stripes for the top ties. For this feature to be shown to its full advantage, you will need a bed without a footboard.

Instead of using two solid colors for the duvet top, you could use harmonizing prints. Broad border prints would emphasize the vertical stripes, while a tiny flowered calico print would also look good and would resemble a solid from a distance. For a coordinated look, choose a print that matches your curtains or pillows.

Whatever combination you choose, remember that the result is most effective when there is a clear contrast, whether of color or pattern, between the stripes.

MATERIALS
For a duvet cover measuring 88in (224cm) square

Cotton for duvet top lighter stripes: 2½yd (2.25m) of 45in (115cm) fabric

Cotton for duvet top darker stripes, ties, and facing: 5yd (4.6m) of 45in (115cm) fabric

Cotton for duvet underside (joined down middle), ties, and facing: 5yd (4.6m) of 45in (115cm) fabric

Black cotton for piping: 1¼yd (1.15m) of 45in (115cm) fabric

Piping cord: 9½yd (8.5m)

Sewing thread matching the colors of the stripes and underside

Duvet top lighter stripe

The Fabrics
A cool, calm harmony of bamboo, ivory, and parchment colors, with a sharp black binding for contrast.

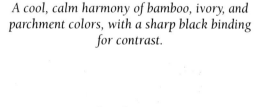
Duvet underside

Duvet top darker stripe

Duvet binding

Making the Duvet Cover

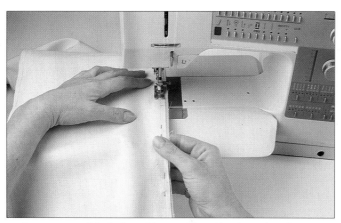

1 *Cut 4 strips of the lighter fabric, each 10½in (27cm) wide, 88¾in (226cm) long, and 5 strips of the darker fabric the same size for the cover top. Pin and stitch right sides of strips together leaving a ⅜in (1cm) seam allowance, alternating light and dark so that a dark strip is on each outside edge.*

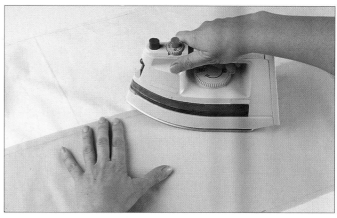

2 *Once you have stitched all 9 strips together, press the 8 seams flat in the direction of the lighter strips.*

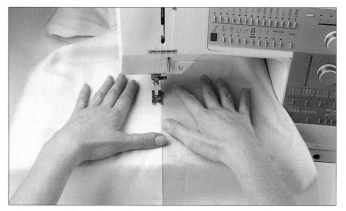

3 *Overstitch on the right side with thread matching the lighter cotton to strengthen the seam and prevent fraying.*

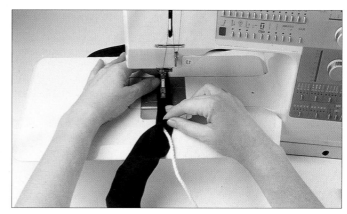

4 *For the piping, cut strips of bias binding 2in (5cm) wide and join them to make one continuous strip at least 30ft (9m) long. Using the zipper foot, stitch around piping cord (see p. 14 for piping and binding techniques).*

5 *To make the ties, cut 6 strips of the darker top fabric, each 2in (5cm) wide, 18½in (47cm) long. Fold them in half lengthwise, turning under the raw edges by ¼in (6mm) down the sides and at the ends and stitch to make ¾in (2cm) wide ties. Pin the piping to the bottom end of the cover top and pin the 6 tie strips over the piping at about 10½in (27cm) intervals.*

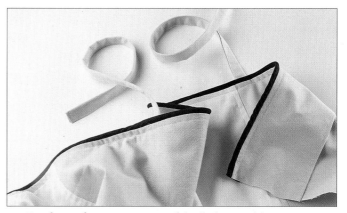

6 *For the top facing, cut a strip of the darker top fabric, 4in (10cm) wide, 88¾in (226cm) long. Pin, baste, and, with the zipper foot, stitch facing to top, right sides together, over the piping and ties. Turn, press, and topstitch as shown. Cut the underside fabric to the same size as the duvet top. Repeat steps 5 and 6 to attach ties and facing to the underside (omitting the piping). Make sure the ties' positions match those on the cover top.*

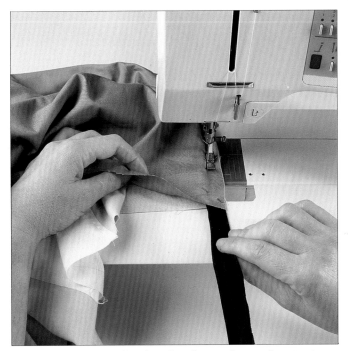

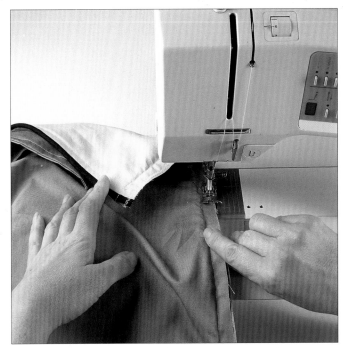

7 *Pin cover top to underside right sides together, with piping in between as shown. Stitch around the remaining 3 sides of the cover with zipper foot, taking special care at the corners, and overstitching the facings at the opening.*

8 *Zigzag stitch around the seam to finish off the inside raw edges. Turn right side out and press. Hand-hem the facings.*

Variation

Savannah Print

Using harmonizing prints for the strips on the duvet top creates a more contemporary look. This combination of chevrons and an animal print, with crisp, natural cotton for the underside, evokes the spirit of Africa and would look good bound in black. Small spots, stripes, florals, or even bold, plain fabric would all offer a nice contrast too.

Duvet top stripe

Duvet underside

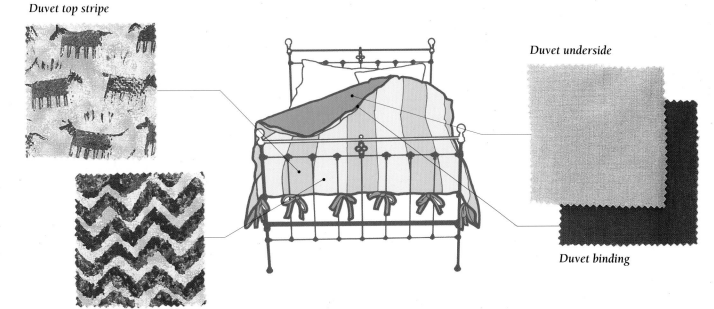

Duvet binding

Duvet top stripe

Alsace Checked Bed Linen

The crisp, clean partnership of red and blue checks, set off by a navy undersheet and natural calico, makes inviting bedding that might have come straight from the wooded valleys of northeast France.

ALSACE IS A HIDDEN CORNER of northeast France that has long been a chief center for producing French textiles such as silk, linen, cotton, and wool. These fabrics range from refined zephyrs and twills to the characteristic homespun cotton and linen Kelsch that has been used for these pillowcases and duvet cover.

As here, Kelsch is usually woven in varying checks of red and white or blue and white, and is nicely set off by cream calico. Together they give an impression of crisp simplicity – and this bedding is simple to make – and a sense of rightness that comes from a classic design.

Small touches such as the contrasting lining and buttonbands allow for an interplay of different colors and checks, lending added definition. The bone-colored buttons punctuate the ends of the pillows and duvet, providing a more stylish closure than common fastenings like plastic press studs.

The dark blue undersheet and matching dark blue and white check cloths covering the bedside table make this a boy's room. However, if you used a white undersheet and lace tablecloth in their place, the duvet cover and pillowcases could look very feminine. Indeed, the style is very adaptable, at home in a modern urban setting or with mellow country pine. Checks, big or small, scarlet or blue, have the great virtue of marrying well.

For a warmer, cozier look, choose two Provençal prints in matching terracotta and cream colors for the duvet cover and pillowcases, with a matching stripe for the buttonbands.

MATERIALS

For two pillowcases measuring 17¾in (45cm) × 27½in (70cm)

Cotton for pillowcases: 2¾yd (2.5m) of 45in (115cm) fabric
Cotton for buttonbands: 1yd (0.8m) of 45in (115cm) fabric
Matching sewing thread
¾in (2cm) buttons: 6
White button thread

For a duvet cover measuring 68in (173cm) × 91½in (232cm)

Cotton for duvet top (joined down middle): 4yd (3.5m) of 45in (115cm) fabric
Cotton for duvet underside (joined down middle): 4yd (3.5m) of 45in (115cm) fabric
Cotton for buttonband (joined down middle): 1yd (0.8m) of 45in (115cm) fabric
Matching sewing thread
¾in (2cm) buttons: 5
Red button thread

The Fabrics

A fresh, classic collection of colors in a familiar but unbeatable partnership. Red, white, and blue always combine well, and bring a bracing gust of seaside air as a positive start to the day.

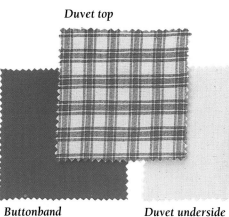

Duvet top

Buttonband

Duvet underside

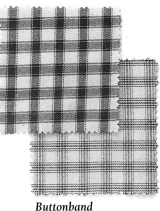

Pillowcase

Buttonband

Making the Pillows and Duvet Cover

The process for making the pillows is shown below. The duvet cover is made in exactly the same way except it requires three seams instead of two since the duvet top and underside consist of two different pieces of fabric. The trim size for the duvet top and underside is 68¾in (175cm) × 88¾in (225cm). The trim size for the two pieces for the buttonband is 7¾in (20cm) × 68¾in (175cm).

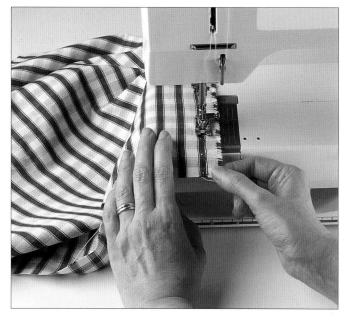

1 *Cut a piece of fabric 18½in (47cm) × 48¾in (124cm) for the pillow and 2 strips 7¾in (20cm) × 18½in (47cm) for the buttonband. Stitch a buttonband strip to each of the 2 short sides of pillowcase fabric, right sides together with a ⅜in (1cm) seam allowance. Press the seams towards the band.*

2 *Fold the pillowcase in half, right sides together. Pin and stitch down each long side of the pillowcase with a ⅜in (1cm) seam allowance. Make sure that the checks in front and back match up and that the band seams are pressed towards the band.*

3 *Zigzag stitch down the raw edges of the 2 long seams to strengthen and neaten. Fold band over to wrong side and pin in place with a ⅜in (1cm) seam allowance, ensuring that band on wrong side is ¼in (6mm) lower than on right side.*

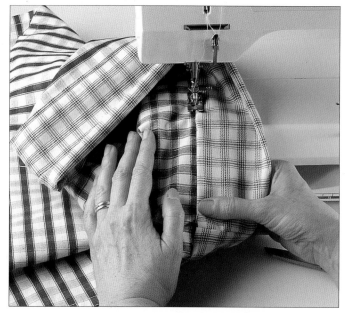

4 *Press band and stitch in a "ditch" from the right side, catching the band beneath. Draw any thread ends through to inside, knot and darn in place. Press. Make buttonholes (see opposite above) and sew buttons in place.*

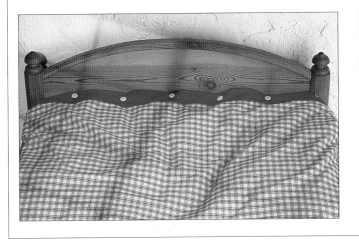

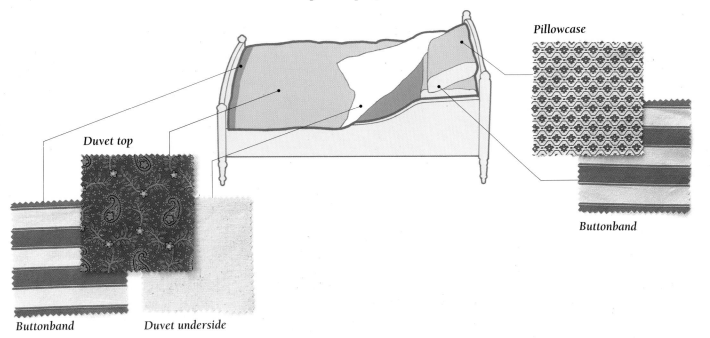

Making Buttonholes

Buttonholes make a tidy closure for pillowcases and duvet covers. If buttonholes are set into an applied band as here, the double thickness of the fabric helps prevent the gaps between the buttons from gaping. The buttonholes for the duvet cover (below) are made in exactly the same way as for the pillows except the duvet cover needs five buttons instead of three because it has a wider opening. See page 14 for techniques on sewing on buttons.

1 Place 3 equidistant buttons along pillowcase band at 4½in (11.5cm) intervals. Pin to mark size and position of buttonholes.

2 Using small stitches, baste around where the buttonhole will be cut to hold the 2 layers of fabric in place and mark the length.

3 With a stitch ripper or sharp embroidery scissors, cut neatly within the basting stitches.

4 Sewing over taut waxed double thread, buttonhole stitch (see p. 11) around sides and overstitch at ends. Pull waxed thread taut and cut away surplus.

Variation

Terracotta and Cream

Two small Provençal prints make lively alternatives for the main fabric of the duvet and pillowcase. The matching stripe used as a buttonband provides a link between the two and gives crisp definition to both.

Pillowcase

Buttonband

Duvet top

Buttonband   *Duvet underside*

Dutch Paisley Duvet Cover

A lavish duvet cover inspired by Dutch quilts of exotically patterned Indian fabrics imported by traders in the seventeenth century.

PAISLEY AND TREE-OF-LIFE designs were first seen in Europe in the fine wood-block printed cottons and silks brought from India by Dutch seafarers. Indian dyers had the secret of mordants that fixed color in the fabric, making the strong, deep, color-fast lines of the imported cloths greatly prized.

Our duvet cover, whose central panel is edged with two bands of contrasting prints, shows how you can combine different, unrelated patterns successfully, provided color and design scale are carefully considered. The bold zigzag stripe contrasts with both the paisley panel and the outer band in a small, allover print. The red in the striped backing fabric echoes the dark red of the paisley motif to create a harmonious whole. Note the finishing touches: the border fabrics are neatly mitered at the corners, which are decorated with golden tassels and piping to complete the exotic Far East look.

The quilt's richness of color and pattern harmonizes beautifully with the ethnic feel of the room's rug and table cover, as well as the warm mahogany bed. But you could take the principle of mixing and matching prints to create quite a different mood. For instance, use the soft antique colors of Jacobean-inspired fabrics to create a medieval feel, or use a combination of patterns in fresh blue and white for a more modern, seaside look. Light, bright shades can look just as striking as deep, rich ones, but remember that you need fairly definite contrasts of tone and pattern so that the final effect looks designed, not haphazard. However, while many manufacturers now offer a range of ready-made coordinating fabrics, the result can look *too* careful. Try choosing your own combinations and be a little daring in deciding what goes together. An element of surprise lifts a decorating scheme out of the ordinary.

MATERIALS

For a duvet cover measuring 88in (224cm) square

Patterned cotton for outer border and facing: 2½yd (2.25m) of 45in (115cm) fabric

Patterned cotton for inner border: 2¼yd (2m) of 45in (115cm) fabric

Patterned cotton for center square: 1⅔yd (1.5m) of 60in (150cm) fabric

Cotton for underside (joined down middle) and facing: 5¼yd (4.6m) of 45in (115cm) fabric

Ready-made gold piping braid: 10yd (9m)

Toggle buttons: 6

Gold braid for button loops: ¼yd (25cm)

Black sewing thread

For tassels

Embroidery thread for tassels: 6 hanks in 3 colors

Gold thread for binding tassels: 3yd (2.75m)

The Fabrics

A paisley design of muted red, brown, and blue is contained inside two different boldly patterned borders, which are harmonized by their black and white color scheme. The red is echoed in the striped underside, adding to the feeling of opulence with its warm tones of yellow ocher.

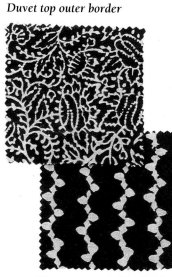

Duvet top outer border

Duvet top center square

Duvet top inner border

Duvet underside

COMPONENTS

Below are the elements needed for an 88in (224cm) square duvet cover

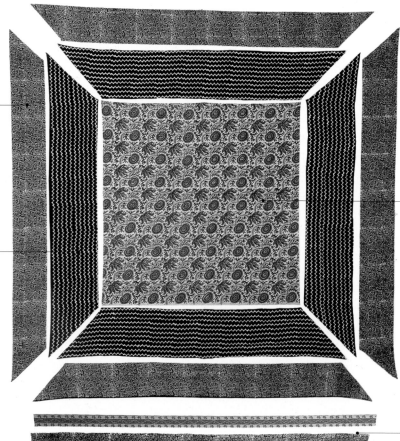

Duvet top outer border:
4 strips, each 7¾in
(19.5cm) wide, 88¾in
(226cm) long, with
ends cut across
diagonally at 45°

Duvet top inner border:
4 strips, each 10⅞in
(27.5cm) wide, 74¾in
(191cm) long, with
ends cut across
diagonally at 45°

Tassels: 6 hanks six-
strand embroidery
thread and gold thread

Duvet top center
square: 54¾in
(140cm) square

Facing for duvet
tops and underside:
each 3in (7.5cm)
wide, 88¾in
(226cm) long

Duvet underside:
88¾in (226cm)
square

Making the Duvet Cover

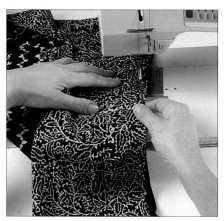

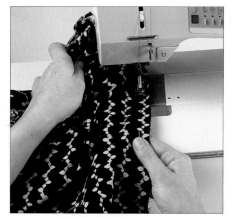

1 Cut all the fabric following the
components photograph. Pin and sew
each outer border of duvet top to its inner
border, right sides together, with ⅜in
(1cm) seams so that when the seams are
pressed open, the edges and the diagonals
at the corners match.

2 Stitch together the bias-cut corners,
matching the seams and taking care
not to stretch the fabric too much (see
p. 12 for mitering techniques). Leave each
inside corner seam open ⅝in (1.5cm) for
attaching center square and overstitch
for strength.

3 Zigzag raw edges of center square and
pin it in position following the
components photograph. Stitch the center
square in place right sides together,
basting it first to make sure of fit. Press all
seams open.

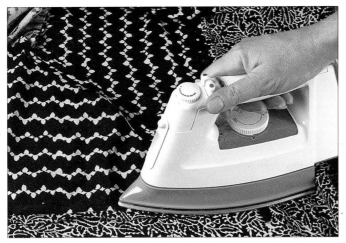

4 Sew facing strip along opening end of duvet underside, right sides together. Turn, press and hem.

5 Along the opening end of the duvet top, baste the piping (see p. 14 for piping techniques), decorative edge facing right side in. Pin loops of gold braid a bit smaller than the length of the toggle to the piping on the duvet top, the loops pointing inwards and their ends sticking out. Here we used 6 loops at 14in (35.5cm) intervals. Overstitch the cut ends of the piping to prevent it from ravelling.

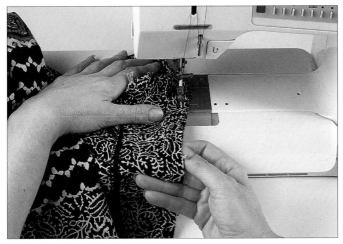

6 Pin facing for duvet top in place, right sides together, with piping in between and all seam edges aligning. Baste in place and stitch, using a zipper foot. Turn right side out, press, and hem.

7 Making sure that the faced opening edges are together, pin the other three sides of the top to the underside, right sides facing, pinning the piping in place as you go and being generous with it at the corners. Overstitch the opening for strength.

8 Turn right side out to check work, then turn inside out again and zigzag stitch all the raw edges together.

9 Mark with a pin or marking pen the positions of the toggles on the duvet underside, making sure they match the positions of the loops.

Making the Duvet Cover (cont.)

10 *Stitch the toggles securely in place using heavy-duty thread or double thickness sewing cotton.*

11 *Stitch on the tassels at the corners (see below for instructions on making tassels).*

Making Tassels

Tassels are one of the simplest ways to add glamour to your sewing. To make the 12 tassels for this duvet, you need 6 hanks of six-strand embroidery thread (a hank makes 2 tassels) and 3 yards (2.75 meters) of gold embroidery thread. Try to get embroidery thread in colors that match those found in the duvet itself.

1 *To make 2 tassels, first knot 2 2in (5cm) lengths of thread to make 2 small loops, leaving enough room on ends for tying.*

2 *Knot the loop ends securely to both ends of a hank of embroidery thread.*

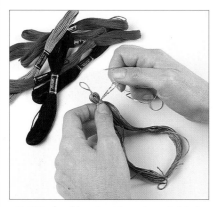

3 *Wind gold embroidery thread tightly around each end of the hank, just below the loop.*

4 *Finish off by stitching the gold thread into the top of the loop securely.*

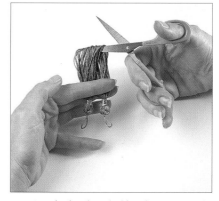

5 *Cut the hank in half to form 2 tassels and trim the cut ends evenly. Repeat the process until you have the required amount of tassels.*

Variations

Study in Blue

For a breezy seaside look, use this combination of fresh blue and white patterns made shipshape by a neat stripe. Here, the center square is in a small print, the outer border in glorious swirling flowers, and the underside in a darker solid blue.

*Duvet front
middle border*

*Duvet front
center square*

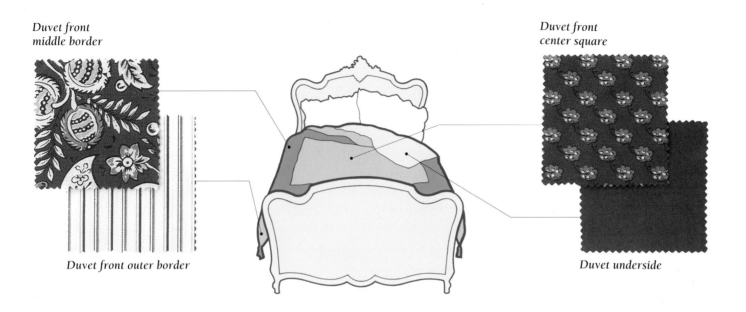

Duvet front outer border

Duvet underside

Four Poster Bedding

Richly patterned, Jacobean-inspired fabrics suit dark, wood surroundings, and these soft antique colors would be ideal dressing for a four-poster bed. The patterned stripe separates the prancing horses decorating the center panel from the magnificent feathers of the outer border. The underside continues the theme with a warm sandy yellow print of small medieval creatures.

*Duvet front
middle border*

*Duvet front
center square*

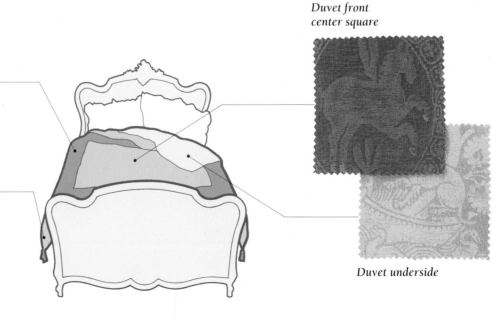

Duvet front outer border

Duvet underside

Flying Geese Quilt

A traditional American design, this quilt is clean, crisp, and easy to make, and the perfect way to recycle scraps rescued from worn clothing.

THE FLYING GEESE MOTIF found its way to America from Great Britain, where it was used along with other border patterns for pieced medallion quilts. It continued to be used in this way in America, but the charm of the triangles chasing each other up the quilt gradually became the main attraction.

Today this quilt is still a wonderful way to make use of worn shirts or other remnants. Vary the patterns of the larger triangles, whether stripes, plaids, flowers, or paisleys, as much as you like, so long as the patterns are a similar scale and there is a unifying color. The design reads best if you confine the small triangles to one paler color and make the stripes from a darker contrast.

If you use solids instead of patterns, however, you can use a mixture of colors. You could use a dark color such as black for both the smaller triangles and stripes and a selection of bright colors for the large triangles, which would stand out against the dark background.

Always keep to the same seam allowance when sewing, because a small error repeated over many triangles will make the plain strips and the flying geese different lengths. However, should this happen, you may be able to rectify this by adding or subtracting a "goose".

If your quilt is for a double bed, broaden it by adding extra strips of flying geese and the other stripe. You could use smaller triangles for a child's bed or crib or simply reduce the amount of strips and the number of flying geese in each strip. Whatever the quilt's size, you do not have to restrict its use to the bed. This heirloom is special enough to hang on your wall.

MATERIALS

For a quilt measuring
76½in (193cm) × 88in (224cm)

Striped cotton for front stripes: 2½yd (2.3m) of 36in (90cm) fabric
Shirting for small triangles: 2¾yd (2.6m) of 36in (90cm) fabric
Shirting for flying geese: 2¾yd (2.6cm) of 36in (90cm) fabric
Striped cotton for underside: 5yd (4.6m) of 45in (115cm) fabric
Plain cotton for binding: 1⅔yd (1.5m) of 45in (115cm) fabric
Batting for interlining: 5yd (4.6m) of 45in (115cm) batting
Red and white sewing thread

The Fabrics

Fine, crisp Egyptian cotton, in myriad stripes of red, white, and blue, spiked with a scarlet binding.

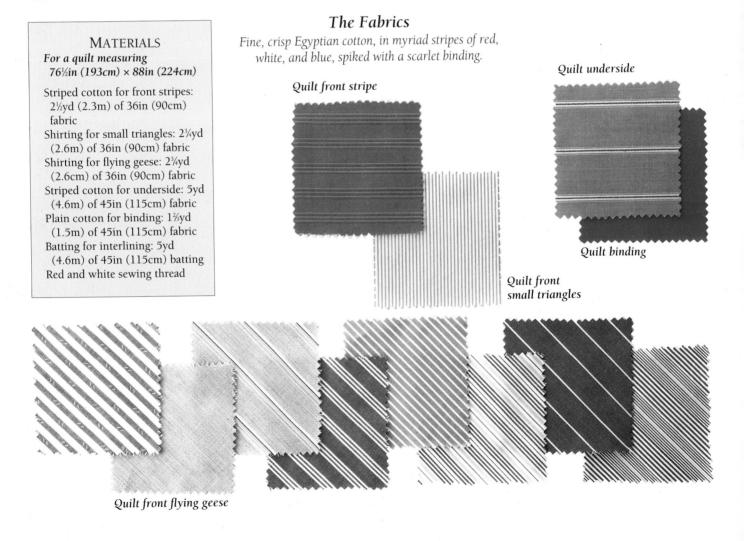

Quilt front stripe

Quilt underside

Quilt binding

Quilt front small triangles

Quilt front flying geese

COMPONENTS

Below are the elements needed for an 88in (224cm) × 76½in (193cm) quilt

Quilt front large flying geese:
90 triangles 11¼in × 8in ×
8in (28.5cm × 20cm × 20cm)
– see template on p. 15

Quilt front small triangles:
180 triangles 8in × 5⅝in ×
5⅝in (20cm × 14cm × 14cm)
– see template on p. 15

Quilt front stripe:
4 strips 6¾in
(17cm) wide, 88¾in
(226cm) long

Quilt underside:
2 strips 39in
(98.5cm) wide ×
88¾in (226cm)
long, to be joined
together.

Binding: 4 2in (5cm) wide strips,
2 strips 89in (226.6cm) long, and
2 strips 77½in (195cm) long

Making the Quilt

1 Using the 2 templates on p. 15, trace and cut 90 large triangles and 180 smaller triangles (see p. 10 for multiple cutting techniques). The templates allow for ⅜in (1cm) seam around each triangle.

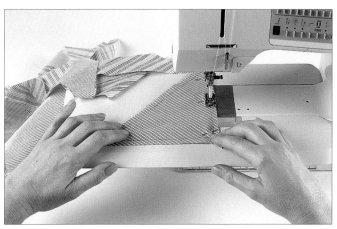

2 Pin and sew the long edge of a small triangle to the shorter edge of a large triangle, right sides together, so that the stripes make a right angle when opened out. Match corners exactly and stitch without stretching the material.

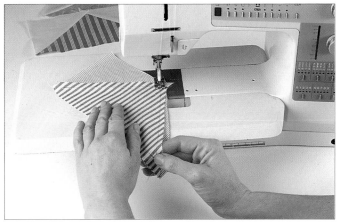

3 Attach the longer edge of another small triangle to the other short edge of the large triangle, right sides together. The point of the large triangle should come ⅜in (1cm) below the top of the resulting rectangle.

4 Repeat the process until all triangles have been combined into rectangles and then press them as shown here.

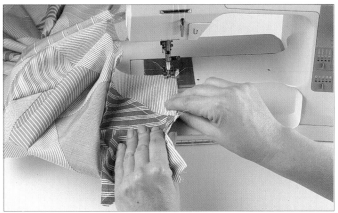

5 Arrange all the rectangles on the floor in the pattern you want (we have gone for a "random" effect). Stitch them right sides together in this arrangement until you have 5 strips of 18 rectangles each. Make sure that the point of the large triangle is exactly on the seam line. Press with points up.

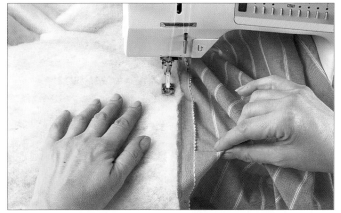

6 Cut the backing material at least 77¼in (195cm) wide and to the same length as the pieced strips (about 88¾in [226cm]). If backing fabric is not wide enough to use in one piece, sew selvage together along center back. Press seam open (or if fabric is in one piece fold in half lengthwise and press fold). Place batting up against center seam (or fold) and pin and stitch.

Making the Quilt (cont.)

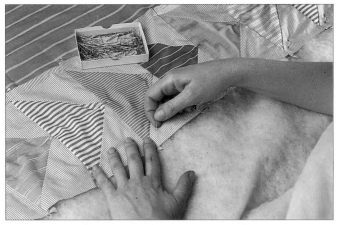

7 Pin a strip of triangles so that triangle points line up over center seam of underside, wrong sides together. Smoothing in place with your hand, pin the outer corners of the triangles in place making sure to go through top, batting, and underside.

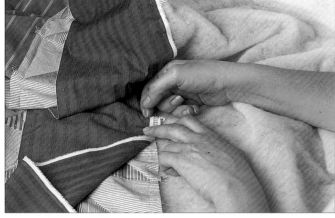

8 Cut the unpieced strips and pin 1 on top of the triangle strip so that right sides are together. To insure accuracy, baste all 4 layers together, checking there are no tucks or wrinkles. Stitch exactly along the outer triangle points.

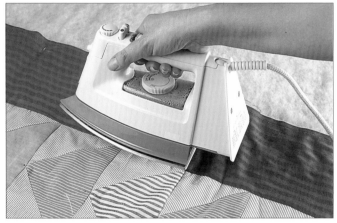

9 Remove basting, turn unpieced strip right side up and press flat, pinning in position as you go. Check both top and underside when you press to ensure that you have not caught any fabric unintentionally.

10 Pin the next strip of triangles in place, following the procedure in steps 8 and 9. Take care that the triangles point in the same direction as the first strip and that the triangles in each strip line up with each other.

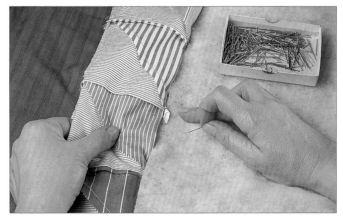

11 Once you have completed sewing together the strips on the first half (3 pieced strips and 2 unpieced strips), place another length of batting up against the center back seam, pinning it in place, and repeat steps 7 through 12 to complete the second half.

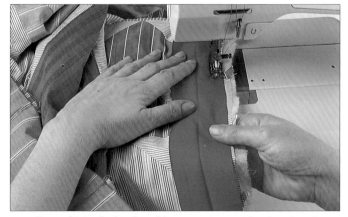

12 Cut and join the binding fabric into 2 strips 2in (5cm) wide, 89in (226.6cm) long (see p. 13 for binding techniques). Press in half lengthwise and pin and sew to sides of quilt, catching top, batting, and underside. Trim excess fabric and batting, turn binding over and hem by hand or machine on other side. Press smooth. Make 2 strips for ends, each 77½in (195cm) long, and repeat the process. At the corners turn under the excess and stitch by hand (see p. 13 for techniques on stitching corners).

Variations

Tiny Prints

Crisp, finely patterned lawn cotton is the perfect fabric for patchwork. Here we have chosen a group of diminutive flower prints in shades of toffee, tan, and tobacco brown, with the broad stripes and small triangles in delicate black and white prints. A rich paisley works well for the underside, and the black binding adds a neat finishing touch.

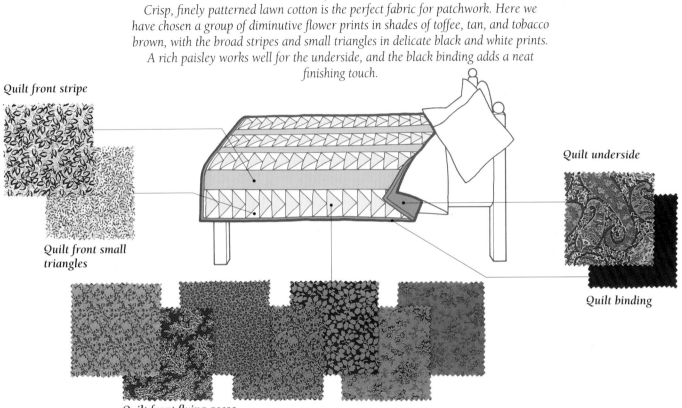

Quilt front stripe

Quilt front small triangles

Quilt underside

Quilt binding

Quilt front flying geese

Amish Plains

A predominance of black was typical of the Amish. Against this background, the bright cottons sing out with full intensity. We have chosen five cottons for the large triangles so that you could use a different color for each strip. A red and white polka dot cotton on the underside picks up the bright red geese on the front.

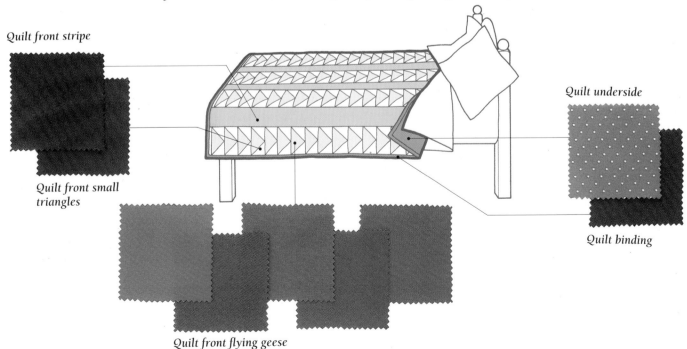

Quilt front stripe

Quilt underside

Quilt front small triangles

Quilt binding

Quilt front flying geese

Shaker Woolen Coverlet

Fleecy wool in a cheering scarlet and black plaid, edged with a broad band of black, makes a cozy coverlet in the handsome, no-nonsense spirit of the Shakers.

THE SPIRIT OF SHAKER workmanship is revived in this warm, comforting coverlet in soft brushed wool. Shaker domestic objects embodied the idea of combining the beautiful with the useful: the humblest utensil displayed perfect proportions, grace of line, and a respectful use of natural materials. Like everything else the Shakers made, their textiles were plain, honest, and good. At the beginning of the nineteenth century they manufactured almost all their own cloth, spinning and weaving a wide variety of natural fibers into an attractive range of striped, plaid, and twill designs. Using raw vegetable materials, they produced colorfast dyes in shades of surprising brilliance.

This blanket is inspired by a Shaker original that had a central panel in gray-green, surrounded by a scarlet, gray, and dark green plaid. The original was backed with red flannel, and the layers – the decorative top, batting, and backing – were tufted with wool yarn.

The technique of stitching through all the layers, then knotting and cutting the thread ends to form a little tassel, is a time-honored method that fulfills the Shaker philosophy of decorativeness combined with practicality. This technique is applicable to any fabric or design.

If the simplicity of the Shaker style appeals, choose a basic woven design rather than prints. Or, for a more lightweight quilt, use cotton instead of wool for the top layer, and match the fabric to curtains or tablecloths in the bedroom. Try a complementary cotton fabric for the border, and tie the blanket layers together with heavy cotton threads.

MATERIALS

For a coverlet measuring 78in (198cm) × 88in (224cm) If you are unable to find 80in (200cm) wide fabric, buy double the length of the coverlet and stitch 2 pieces together

Checked wool for front: 2½yd (2.3m) of 80in (200cm) fabric
Red wool for backing: 2½yd (2.3m) of 80in (200cm) fabric
Wool flannel for interlining: 2½yd (2.3m) of 80in (200cm) fabric
Black wool for binding: 2yd (1.85m) of 45in (115cm) fabric
Cream double knitting wool for tufting: 10yd (9m)
Black sewing thread

The Fabrics

An extroverted scarlet and black plaid with a discreet thread of cream echoed by the tufting. It has been edged with black and has a soft scarlet backing.

Coverlet front

Coverlet backing

Coverlet binding

Making the Coverlet

1 *Cut out the fabric for the front, interlining, and backing, all at least 74in (188cm) × 84in (214cm). Lay out interlining over backing fabric, stretching it to fit. Next lay checked wool on top and pin all 3 layers together.*

2 *After making sure that the surface is flat and even, pin and baste around the edges.*

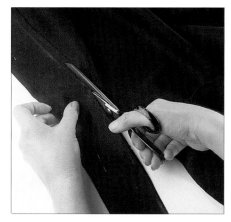

3 *For the binding, cut binding fabric into strips 5½in (14cm) wide (see p. 13 for binding techniques) and join strips together to make 4 strips, 2 at least 74in (188cm) long for the ends and 2 at least 88½in (225cm) long for the sides.*

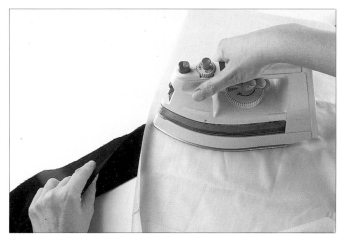

4 *Using a damp cloth to protect the wool, press the joining seams of the strips open. Then press the binding in half lengthwise.*

5 *Take the 2 shorter strips of binding and sew one to the head and one to the foot of the coverlet, right sides facing with a ⅜in (1cm) seam allowance.*

6 *Trim any excess fabric, turn binding right side over, and hem by machine on backing side. Press.*

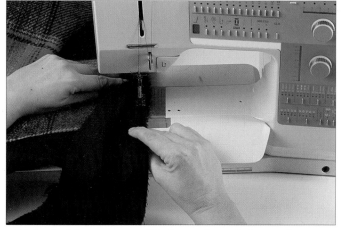

7 *Take the 2 longer strips of binding and attach them to the edges in the same way, turning under a small hem at each end (see p. 13 for techniques on stitching corners).*

8 Overstitch the corners by machine, both to neaten and strengthen the coverlet (see p. 13 for techniques on stitching corners).

9 Mark positions for hand-tied tufting with pins. We have used the check to make a diamond pattern, spacing the tufts at about 10in (25cm) intervals. Stitch through the whole coverlet with a double length of double knitting wool. Knot the ends securely with a reef knot (see p. 11) and cut the wool to 1in (2.5cm), teasing it out to fluff up the fibers.

Variation

Indian Ikat

The Shaker coverlet adapts well to a wide range of fabrics and looks. Here, thick Ikat cotton's flame pattern is echoed in hot colors – red on the front and toffee brown on the back, bound in scarlet, making an attractive summer quilt.

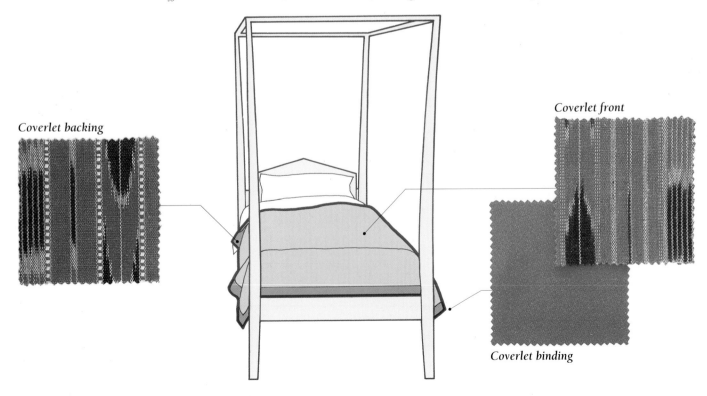

Coverlet backing

Coverlet front

Coverlet binding

Tartan Baby Quilt

*Infant chic in strong colors bestrewn with scarlet hearts – this
is for a modern baby who cannot resist a nod to nostalgia.*

THIS BABY QUILT is quick and fun to make, but will probably inspire a lifelong devotion in its owner's heart. This crib-sized quilt has the handsome good looks of classic bedclothing. The cotton and polyester components can be washed and dried, so that spills and stains are easily cleaned. In addition, it is light and packable and a comforting little bit of home for a baby to take away on visits.

For maximum impact, we have restricted the plaids to three basic, strong colors – red, white, and blue – that are linked by their secondary color, green. The scarlet used for the heart motifs and borders brightens the look, and the narrow navy blue binding gives the quilt its distinct edge. Of course, you can vary the colors to pick up the main color themes in the room for which the quilt is intended, echoing the colors of walls, floors, or curtains.

For a softer effect, choose small, all-over floral prints in contrasting shades or substitute pastels for primaries. Other motifs – Scottie dogs, bows, or Sunbonnet Sues, for example – could replace the hearts, or personalize the quilt by appliquéing the baby's name onto symmetrical squares, using the alphabet template on page 17.

Bear in mind that your work of art will get plenty of hard wear. It will be chewed, dragged along the ground, and even wrapped around the dog, so finish it carefully, avoiding buttons and loose threads. Your care will be rewarded; in only an afternoon's sewing, you will have created an enduring piece of family memorabilia.

MATERIALS
*For a baby's quilt measuring
28in (70cm) × 39in (100cm)*

Red and green plaid shirting for
front squares: ⅔yd (50cm) of
45in (115cm) fabric
Blue and green plaid shirting for
front squares: ⅔yd (50cm) of
45in (115cm) fabric
White and red plaid shirting for
front squares: ⅔yd (50cm) of
45in (115cm) fabric
Red cotton shirting for underside
and hearts: 1⅔yd (1.5m) of 36in
(90cm) fabric
Navy cotton shirting for piping:
⅔yd (50cm) of 36in (90cm)
fabric
Piping cord: 4½yd (4m)
Lightweight batting: 1yd (90cm)
of 45in (115cm) batting
Red chenille for outlining hearts:
2½yd (2.25m)
Paper-backed adhesive web for
attaching appliquéd hearts
Red and navy sewing thread

The Fabrics
*Plaids, predominantly red, green, blue, and white,
machine-quilted onto a rich red underside, and
narrowly bound in navy blue.*

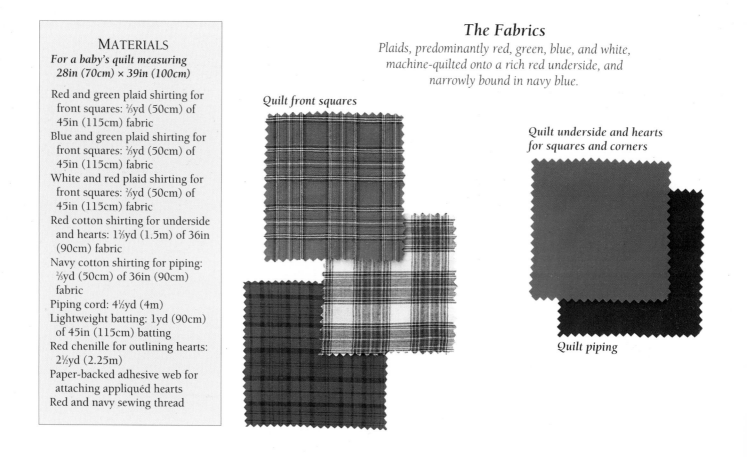

Quilt front squares

*Quilt underside and hearts
for squares and corners*

Quilt piping

COMPONENTS

Below are the elements needed for a 28in (70cm) × 39in (100cm) quilt

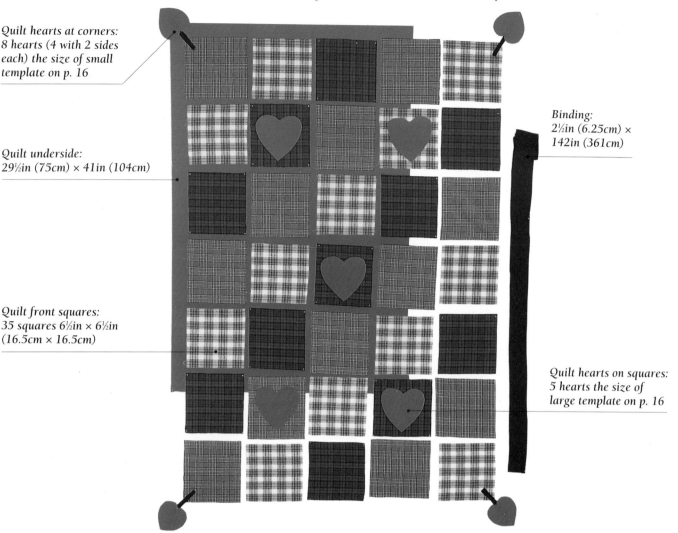

Quilt hearts at corners:
8 hearts (4 with 2 sides
each) the size of small
template on p. 16

Binding:
2½in (6.25cm) ×
142in (361cm)

Quilt underside:
29½in (75cm) × 41in (104cm)

Quilt front squares:
35 squares 6½in × 6½in
(16.5cm × 16.5cm)

Quilt hearts on squares:
5 hearts the size of
large template on p. 16

Making the Quilt

1 Cut out 35 squares following
components guide (see p. 10 for
multiple cutting techniques). Using the
large heart template on p. 16, cut 5 hearts
out of the scarlet fabric.

2 Using the same template, cut 5 hearts
out of paper-backed adhesive web and
iron 1 to the wrong side of each heart.

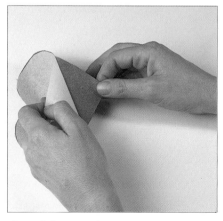

3 Peel the paper backing from the
adhesive web, revealing the adhesive
surface.

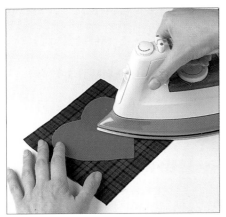

4 *Iron hearts onto the center of 3 dark, 1 medium, and 1 light tartan square, following the components guide.*

5 *Zigzag stitch hearts onto squares over thick red wool or chenille yarn for extra definition. Pin the wool or yarn in position first for accuracy. You will need about 17in (43cm) of yarn for each heart.*

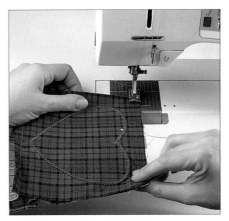

6 *Sew squares together, right sides facing and with a ⅜in (1cm) seam, into strips of 7 squares each. Arrange them following the components photograph. Press seams open.*

7 *Sew strips together, right sides facing and with a ⅜in (1cm) seam, using the components photograph as a guide. Be careful to match square seams as you proceed.*

8 *Once you have finished the top cover, press it thoroughly, seams open, on the wrong side.*

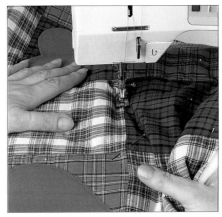

9 *Pin or baste batting to the back of the quilt. Sew along all seams using straight stitch or zigzag stitch.*

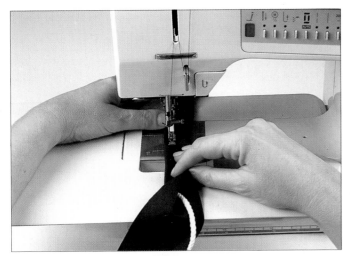

10 *For the piping, cut binding fabric into strips 2½in (6.25cm) wide and join together to make a strip at least 142in (361cm) long (see p. 13 for binding techniques). Press seams of binding open and sew around piping cord using zipper foot and matching dark blue thread (see p. 14 for piping techniques).*

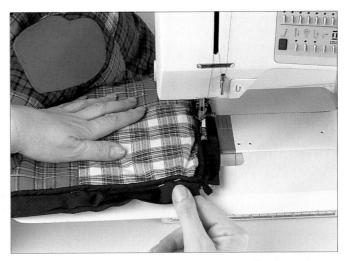

11 *Pin or baste piping in position around edges of quilt top (see p. 14 for piping techniques). Clip corners for ease. Stitch in place using zipper foot, leaving a few inches unsewn at both ends.*

Making the Quilt (cont.)

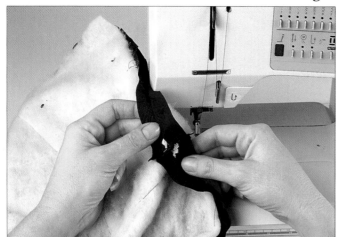

12 *Cut piping cord where it meets and hand sew strips together. Stitch the last few inches to the quilt.*

13 *Having attached corner hearts (see step 6 of Making the Hearts), cut quilt underside following components photograph and pin in place being sure to catch top, batting, and underside. Hem in position by hand, with a seam allowance of ⅜in (1cm).*

Making the Hearts

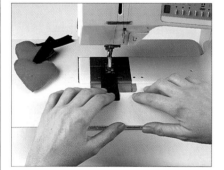

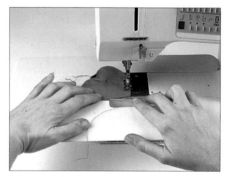

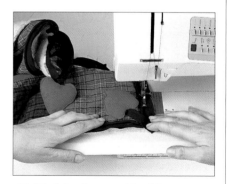

1 *Cut out 8 strips of navy binding, 1½in (3.75cm) wide, 2in (5cm) long. Fold in half lengthwise and hem by machine ¼in (0.5cm) from edge. Turn inside out.*

2 *Using the small heart template on p. 16, cut out 8 hearts (see p. 10 for multiple cutting techniques) and pin pairs right sides together with navy strips inside. Stitch around edges, only stitching navy strip in place at the top. Leave a 1in (2.5cm) opening at the bottom.*

3 *After making the hearts, clip the tops carefully up to the seam to make it lie better when it is turned the right side out.*

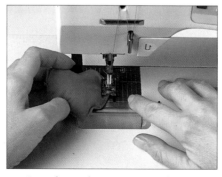

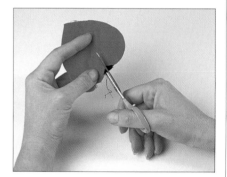

4 *Turn hearts right side out and stuff the hearts with fluffed-up batting.*

5 *Straight stitch or zigzag stitch around the outside edge.*

6 *Stitch in place on side of the piping facing the underside. The underside will cover up the ends of the strips when it is hemmed on top of them in step 13.*

Variations

Freehand Flowers

These lively, hand-drawn designs in cool blues achieve a refined look. The underside is a similar print in invigorating red, and the dark blue piping punctuates the edge and links the two sides of the quilt together. An alternative to hearts might be the owner's initials in bold blue appliquéd to the top.

Quilt front squares

Quilt underside

Quilt piping

Honeysuckle and Roses

This enchanting combination of rosebuds and nosegays in shades of pink, white, and gray cotton is lovely for a baby girl's crib. Five honeysuckle sprigs cut from coordinating fabric are appliquéd in place of hearts. The piping is plain pink and the underside candy-striped pink and white sprinkled with roses.

Quilt front squares

Quilt underside

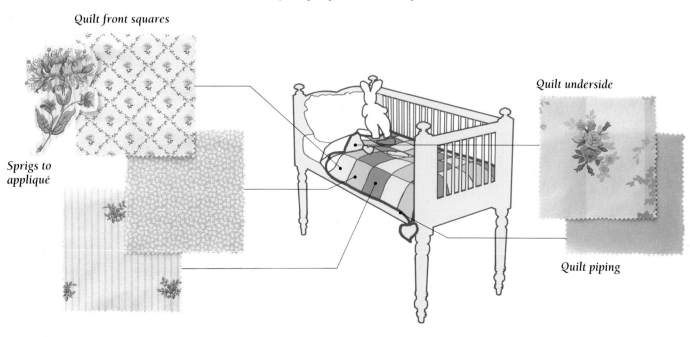

Sprigs to appliqué

Quilt piping

CURTAINS

Seaside Stripe Curtains

Three variations of blue and white ticking and stripes combine in a fresh window treatment that recalls the crisp, clean spirit of a seaside holiday.

THE INFALLIBLE CHARM of blue and white has been exploited since Byzantine and Ming potters first used the combination in the fourteenth century. In these charming curtains and shade, the warm white of unbleached cotton marries perfectly with the rich cobalt of indigo-dyed cloth, which improves as it fades and ages, creating a relaxed nautical look. The three different classic stripes have impact enough without embellishment. Small details like a shell in place of a shade pull, horizontally striped loops, and the navy zigzag stitching around the bottom and side hems of the shade add distinction. The stitching also helps to flatten the side hems so they do not bulk up on the roller. An optional cotton lace border on the shade adds a note of softness to the otherwise crisp mixture.

These curtains and shade fit in with the simplicity of the wooden walls and floors, giving a breezy, summery feel, but this simple formula works well in endless permutations. For a romantic look, make chintz curtains awash with roses, tied back with a darker chintz in a simpler, coordinating design, and accented with a crisp shade of shirting cotton, finished with chunky cream lace. Or, use blue and gold swirls, tied back with a check in matching colors and further brightened by a yellow damask shade with a plain blue border. On a tall window you could also use the check for a cornice or hem border to add a crisp finish. To provide a stronger link between the curtains and the shade, use the plain blue border fabric to vertically edge the curtains.

We have used a roller shade because its simple mechanics are well suited to the limited space available behind the curtains, but you could also use a Roman shade, which pulls up in horizontal folds, if there is room for it behind the curtains.

MATERIALS

For a pair of curtains to fit a window measuring 38in (96.5cm) × 56in (142cm), 30in (76cm) from the floor.

Fabric for curtains: 3yd (2.7m) of 60in (150cm) fabric
White sewing thread
Curtain rod to measure

For two tie-backs, each 27in (69cm) long
Fabric for tie-backs: ½yd (46cm) of 60in (150cm) fabric
Four shells
White sewing thread

For a shade 38½in (98cm) × 79in (200cm)
Stiff cotton fabric: 2¼yd (2.05m) of 45in (115cm) fabric
Cotton lace: 1¼yd (1.1m) of 2in (5cm) lace
Navy blue sewing thread
White sewing thread
Roller shade kit to measure
Cord: 1yd (90cm)
Brass hardware for cord
Shell for cord

The Fabrics

A classic combination of colors that will never fall from grace – variations on a blue and white theme, with stripes of different width in close-weave cotton.

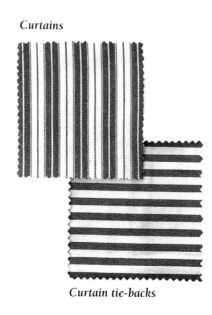

Curtains

Curtain tie-backs

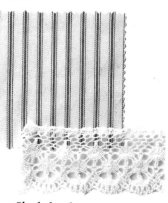

Shade

Shade border

Making the Curtains

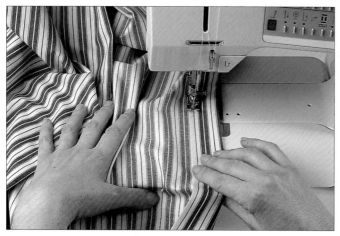

1 *Measure and cut the fabric for the curtains (see p. 8 for measuring techniques), allowing for a 1½in (3.75cm) seam on each side. Cut 2 separate facing strips to the same width and 2½in (6.25cm) deep. Stitch a seam 1½in (3.75cm) wide down both sides of the first curtain.*

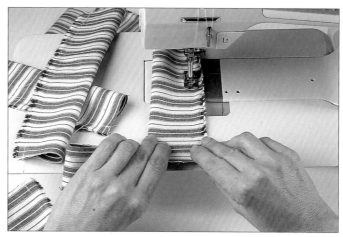

2 *To make curtain loops, cut 12 bands (6 for each curtain) from the same fabric as the curtain, each 5in (12.5cm) wide, 10in (25cm) long. Stitch them into cylinders by folding each in half right sides together, and sewing along their long edges with a ½in (1.25cm) seam allowance.*

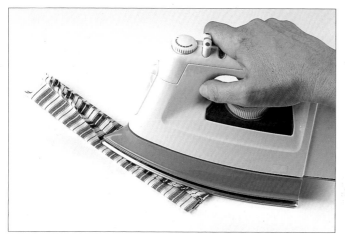

3 *Position each band so that the seam runs down the center and press the seam open.*

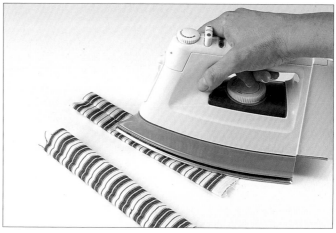

4 *Turn the bands right side out and press again along the seam to make sure the seams are lying flat.*

5 *Fold bands in half, seam side inward, and, with the raw edges aligned at the top, pin 1 to the front of each end of the curtain. Measure equidistant positions for the remaining 4 bands (here 8¼in [21cm] apart) and pin them in place.*

6 *Pin facing strip along the top of the curtain right sides together, over the bands. Stitch along the top leaving a ½in (1.25cm) seam allowance.*

7 *Turn facing over to wrong side. Turn it under and pin a ½in (1.25cm) edge along the length and at the ends, maintaining an even depth.*

8 *Stitch along the length and ends of the facing to secure both the facing and the bands to the curtain.*

9 *Turn up and pin a hem to required length (trim excess fabric if hem is more than 6in [15cm]). Stitch down 1 edge of the hem, across the width and up the other edge. The stitches are visible so the line must be straight. Use a line of basting stitches or a chalk line to guide you if needed. Repeat the whole process for second curtain and hang curtains.*

Making the Tie-backs

To make the two tie-backs, cut two strips of fabric, each 9in (23cm) × 60in (150cm). Stitch them into cylinders as in step 2 of *Making the Curtains*, but make sure to leave an unsewn gap of about 6in (15cm) in the middle for turning right side out. Press the seams open as in step 3 of *Making the Curtains* and stitch a shallow "v" (our "v" is 1½in [3.75cm] deep) from the sides to a point in the middle seam at either end. Trim off the excess fabric outside the "v" and turn right side out.

Tease out the points at either end with a knitting needle by pushing outwards from the inside. Press carefully as in step 4 of *Making the Curtains*, turning under the unstitched edges of the long seam, and slipstitch (see p. 11) invisibly together.

To attach the shells, drill a small hole at the end of each of the shells and sew one to the point at each end of the tie-backs. Sew a loop or ring to the center of each tie-back to attach them to a wall hook.

Making the Shade

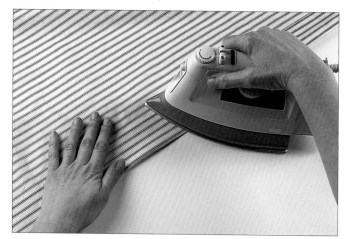

1 Measure and cut the fabric for the shade (see pp. 8–10 for measuring and cutting techniques), allowing for a 2in (5cm) hem on each side, 1in (2.5cm) for attaching the shade to the roller, and 2⅛in (5.4cm) for the bottom hem.

2 Turn back and press 2in (5cm) hems on each side of the shade. After pressing, pinning is not necessary.

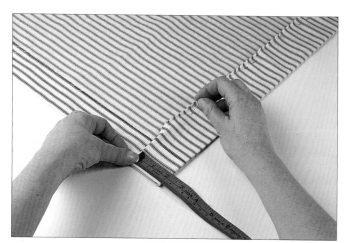

3 Zigzag stitch down hems in navy blue, following a stripe or pattern if there is one, to keep the stitching line straight. If there is not, mark a guiding line first since the stitching will be visible.

4 Along the bottom edge, turn up and pin a 2in (5cm) hem with a ⅛in (4mm) seam allowance and press to provide a crease along what will be the bottom of the shade when the hem is stitched.

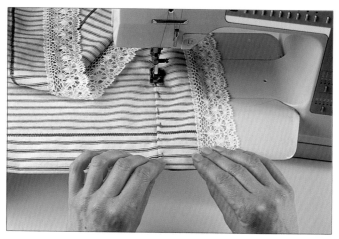

5 Unpin hem and pin and stitch the straight edge of lace onto the hem side of the crease. This means that when the hem is repinned and stitched, the stitching attaching the lace to the shade will be invisible from the front.

6 Pin the hem back up and zigzag stitch along its length in navy blue, leaving the ends open to insert the wooden lath. Attach the top of the shade to the roller following the instructions in the kit.

Variations

Provençal Roses

Surprising, slightly offbeat color combinations are successful when they appear in well coordinated designs such as these for the curtain and tie-back. The curtains would look good very full, possibly draped around the curtain pole. The shade is of crisp, finely striped shirting cotton, finished with chunky cream lace.

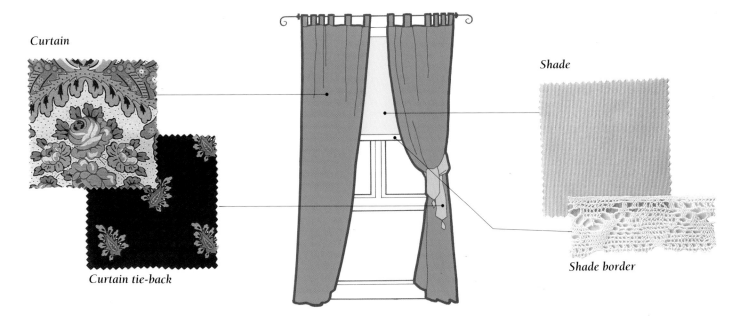

Curtain

Curtain tie-back

Shade

Shade border

Blue and Gold Swirls

With a perfect color match, you can mix the swirling design of the curtain fabric with the checks of the tie-back. On a tall window, you could also use the check for a cornice or hem border to add a crisp finish. The yellow damask shade will always look sunny and is finished neatly with a border of plain blue.

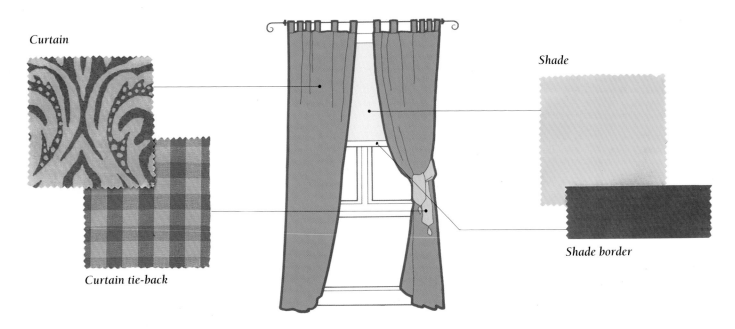

Curtain

Curtain tie-back

Shade

Shade border

Café Curtain

*As simple as can be – sage green and slate blue checks
on hand-woven cotton, distinguished by a scalloped top
and shiny brass rings – this curtain allows the best of both
worlds, all the light you could need and the privacy
you want.*

CAFÉ CURTAINS ARE the simplest, most versatile way of letting in light while preserving privacy. Seen here, they fit in perfectly with the casual simplicity of the room. Note how the sage green of the checks picks up the color of the window frame, sill, and chair rail, while the natural cotton color reflects the warm cream of the walls. The decorative scallops along the top edge of the curtain add extra interest and fit in with the geometric design of the fabric. You can adapt their size to suit the fabric you choose.

The curtain pole can be brass as shown, wood, or, for a rustic look, bamboo. We have positioned it so that the curtain covers slightly more than half the window. Adapt the height according to your needs; higher for more privacy or lower to let in more light.

You can use café curtains in any room in your home. Vary the style and color of the fabric you choose so that it suits the room for which it is intended. For a kitchen or dining room you could use berry-covered gold cotton or some other pattern with a fruit theme. In a study, striped ticking matching the color scheme of the room would be ideal.

The basic concept of the café curtain is so simple that any fabric – solid or sheer, dark or light, plaid, striped, or floral – is perfectly suitable. With café curtains, endless moods and permutations are possible.

MATERIALS
For a café curtain to fit a window measuring 38in (96.5cm) × 56in (142cm)

Coarse hand-woven cotton for curtain: 1½yd (1.4m) of 60in (150cm) fabric
Matching sewing thread
Brass curtain pole with brass rings

The Fabric
Sage green, slate blue, and natural white cotton, enlivened with a narrow stripe of butterscotch brown, echoing the classic colors of Shaker interiors and well-ordered peace and calm.

Curtain

Making the Curtain

1 *Measure and cut out the fabric for curtain (see pp. 8–10 for measuring and cutting techniques), allowing 7in (18cm) in all for top and bottom hems. Fold over 3½in (9cm) at the top of the fabric and press. Using the template on p. 16 or one of your own devising, draw evenly spaced semicircles across folded top of the curtain. Leave at least 1in (2.5cm) between each semicircle and 1¾in (4.5cm) at each end.*

2 *Pin ⅜in (1cm) around the outside of the semicircles and at both ends of facing (leaving ¾in [2cm] seam allowance), to hold facing in place. Stitch around semicircles and at both ends of facing.*

3 *Remove pins and cut out semicircles, leaving a ⅜in (1cm) seam allowance.*

4 *Using sharp embroidery scissors, make small slashes in the seam allowance at 1½in (4cm) intervals, taking care not to cut the stitching.*

5 *Trim the top corners at a 45° angle at both ends of the top hem outside the seam allowance. This will reduce the bulk when the curtain is turned right side out.*

6 *Turn the top hem right side out and tease out the points with a blunt needle. Pin top hem with a ⅜in (1cm) seam allowance and stitch.*

7 *Pin up bottom hem edges to desired length on front side of curtain, with a ⅜in (1cm) seam allowance at the top and a ¾in (2cm) seam allowance at each side. Stitch the sides of the hem, creating a pocket.*

8 *Turn bottom hem right side out. Pin ¾in (2cm) hems along both sides of curtain and stitch the hems all the way around.*

9 *Sew the rings by hand to the back of the semicircle points at the top of the curtain. All that should be visible from the front are the rings themselves.*

Variations

Summer Fruit

This berry-covered gold cotton would be a perfect choice for a kitchen or dining room. Since the fabric is lighter, it would be a good idea to make the curtains somewhat fuller.

Ticking

Ticking is a beautiful, inexpensive, and easy-to-use fabric. In this chic combination of navy and gold, it would be handsome in a study window.

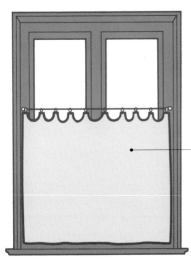

Curtain

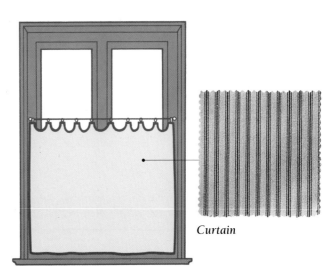

Curtain

Striped Pieced Curtains

*Brilliant colors to wake up any décor: three different striped
versions of lightweight, woven cotton create dazzling curtains
lined in sunshine yellow.*

STRONG, VIBRANT COLORS stand up beautifully to the dazzling brilliance of sunlight in tropical climates. In cooler climates, primary shades are also very effective, lifting the mood of a room on the darkest day.

Inspired by the vivid colors of ethnic textiles from Guatemala, we have made these generously sized curtains from three striped fabrics in different weaves but related tones. They are joined horizontally to add distinction and give a feeling of width to the window. This allows fullness without vertical seaming. They are finished with a facing at the bottom, which acts like a false hem, adding extra weight to the curtains to ensure that they hang well.

The bright yellow lining is attached to the curtain by two lines of stitching along the top, creating an open pocket through which you slide the curtain pole. The fit around the pole should be tight so that the curtains stay bunched up when pulled back as here, but not so tight that you have difficulty closing them (see *Hanging the Curtains* on page 68). Below the pole the lining hangs free like a second curtain. The effect, particularly when billowed out by a gust of wind, feels reminiscent of a warm tropical breeze.

Note how the painted window frame picks up the blue stripe in the curtains. You can pick your fabric so that its colors match the dominant colors of an existing decorative scheme, or perhaps the bright colors of these curtains will inspire you to repaint a window or even an entire room!

You can adapt the pieced design to create very different results. Use exuberant cotton prints with charming flora and fauna designs for a child's bedroom. Alternatively, vary the width of the strips and combine two fine linens with an open-weave braid to give a more subdued and sophisticated effect.

MATERIALS

*For a pair of curtains to fit a
window measuring 42in (107cm)
× 60in (152cm), 18in (46cm)
from the floor.*

Striped cotton for narrow strips
and facing: 2⅛yd (2.05m) of
60in (150cm) fabric
Striped cotton for medium strips:
2⅛yd (2.05m) of 60in (150cm)
fabric
Striped cotton for broad strips:
2yd (2.13m) of 60in (150cm)
fabric
Cotton for lining: 6yd (5.5m) of
60in (150cm) fabric
Matching sewing thread
Curtain pole to measure

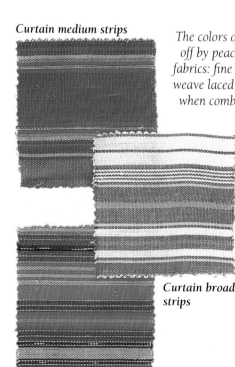

Curtain medium strips

*Curtain broad
strips*

Curtain narrow strips

The Fabrics

*The colors of mango, watermelon, and guava, set
off by peacock blue and green in three different
fabrics: fine stripes, wide stripes, and an irregular
weave laced with plenty of white – an electric mix
when combined with the sunshine yellow lining.*

Curtain lining

COMPONENTS
Below are the elements needed for a 46in (117cm) × 87in (221cm) curtain.
Duplicate the components below for the second curtain

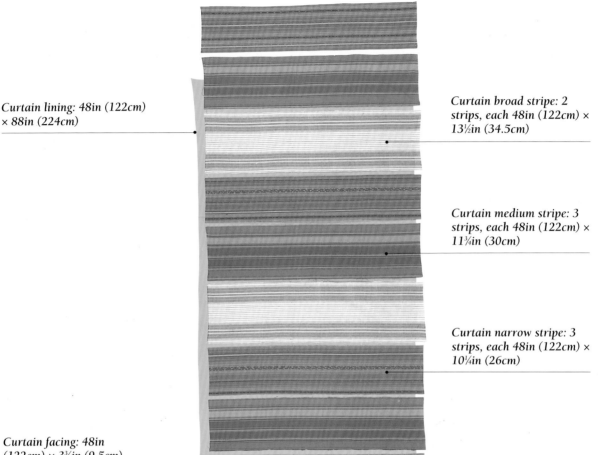

Curtain lining: 48in (122cm) × 88in (224cm)

Curtain broad stripe: 2 strips, each 48in (122cm) × 13½in (34.5cm)

Curtain medium stripe: 3 strips, each 48in (122cm) × 11¾in (30cm)

Curtain narrow stripe: 3 strips, each 48in (122cm) × 10¼in (26cm)

Curtain facing: 48in (122cm) × 3¾in (9.5cm)

Making the Curtains

1 Measure, cut, and lay out all the strips of fabric for both curtains following the components photograph. Having checked that they match each other, pin the strips (but not the facing) right sides together, so every lower strip slightly overlaps the strip above it.

2 Take the fabric for the first curtain and stitch all the strips together, so every lower strip has a seam allowance of ⅜in (1cm) and every upper strip of ½in (1.25cm).

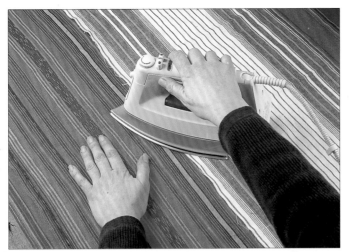

3 Press all the seams towards the top of the curtain so that the wider seam allowance covers the narrower one. This is so you can stitch flat-fell seams along each strip.

4 Turn the edges of the wider seam allowances under the narrower ones and stitch to make flat-fell seams (see p. 12) which should all be ⅜in (1cm) wide.

5 Lay the curtain over the lining right sides together, and stitch along the top edge only, with a ⅜in (1cm) seam allowance (the lining hangs free from the curtain at the sides).

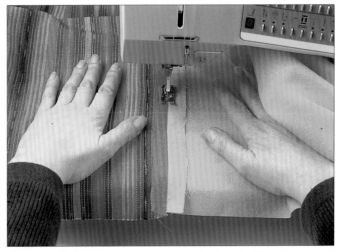

6 Press the seam open and zigzag stitch along it. This flattens and strengthens the join.

7 Pin the facing to the bottom of the curtain right sides together. Stitch it to the curtain along the bottom and at the sides with a ⅜in (1cm) seam allowance, creating a pocket.

8 Turn the facing right side out, press it, and pin it to the curtain along the top edge of the facing.

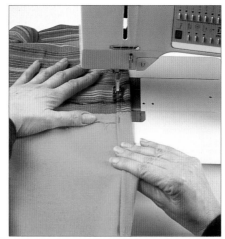

9 *Starting at one of the top corners, pin a ⅜in (1cm) hem and zigzag stitch with yellow thread down the side of the curtain. When you reach the facing, zigzag stitch along it and then go up the other side to the top.*

10 *After checking that it matches the curtain for length, repeat the process for the lining, making a ⅜in (1cm) hem along the sides and bottom.*

11 *Zigzag stitch through the curtain and the lining across the top, leaving a channel wide enough to encircle the curtain pole (see below). Repeat steps 2–11 to make the second curtain.*

Hanging the Curtains

It is essential that the channel at the top of the curtain is exactly the right size for the circumference of the pole. It should be tight enough for the curtains to stay bunched when they are pulled back, but loose enough for the curtains to be easily closed. To achieve this, make the channel about ½ inch (1.25cm) bigger than the circumference of the pole. This pole has a circumference of 3½ inches (8.75cm) so we zigzag stitched 2 inches (5cm) down from the top seam, creating a channel 4 inches (10cm) wide. Ensure that your pole is smooth so that the curtain runs easily along it.

Variations

Birds and Flowers

Exuberant cotton prints of sky-blue and yellow, in charmingly childish flora and fauna designs, are lined with cobalt blue cotton. The curtains would be ideal for a child's bedroom, but could also suit any room hungry for pattern and color.

Curtain broad strips

Curtain narrow strips

Curtain lining

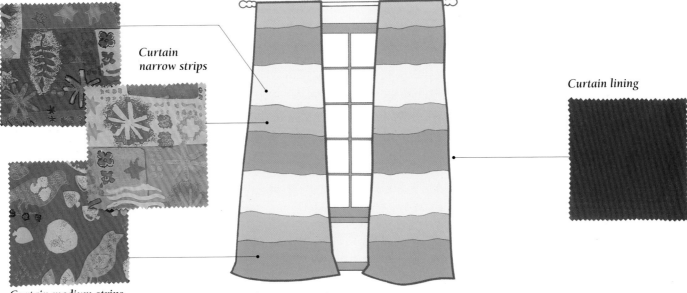

Curtain medium strips

Driftwood Linen

For a different effect, vary the width of the strips. Here open-weave braid separates two transparently fine linens – one in delicate stripes and the other in cleverly woven checks. A cream handkerchief linen for the lining adds to the subtle mixture that would enhance a room with white walls, minimal furnishings, and a floor of bare wooden boards.

Curtain broad strips

Curtain narrow strips

Curtain lining

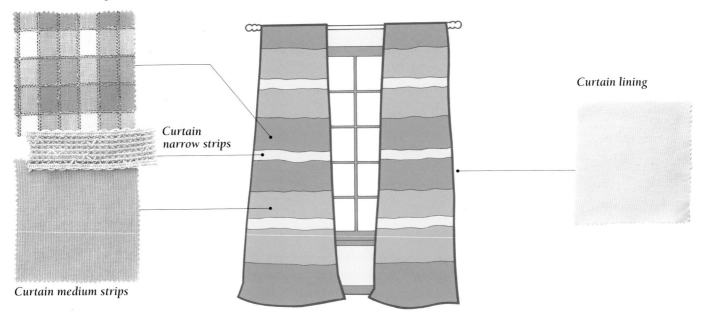

Curtain medium strips

Kilim Print Door Curtain

A heavy, lined door curtain gives a look of baronial splendor to the plainest entrance, and keeps out the draft on wintry evenings.

DOOR CURTAINS ARE not used often anymore, which is a pity, since they add a sense of warmth and grandeur, and are terrific at keeping out the draft. A door curtain's size makes it possible to exploit large, dramatic designs such as the handsome Turkish kilim rug motif shown here. And, because door curtains are meant to be seen from both sides – particularly if they are used as room dividers or across an arch – you can experiment with contrasting textiles. Here, the red of the ticking picks up the red in the kilim design, and its crisp neatness is a nice contrast to the opulent kilim pattern.

Ensure that the curtain is at least one and a half times the width of the door (including frame). It should not hang in overly generous folds since this makes leaving or entering the room awkward, but it should easily extend beyond the door frame when drawn across and clear the top of the door molding by at least an inch

(2.5cm). You can buy curtain rails that attach to the door so that both the door and curtain open at once. These are particularly useful if the door is in constant use. However, these rods are not usually as attractive as a wrought iron or mahogany pole.

If you use a simple pole and rings as here, it is essential that the rings slide easily along the pole. Whatever you choose, ensure that the curtain hangs to the floor to exclude drafts, but is not so long that it will catch under the door when it is opened.

Here, we have used a pair of antique tassels as tie-backs, but you could use whatever you want. As shown on page 74, you could braid together leftovers of the fabric you used to make the curtains.

This curtain design can easily be used in other ways as well. Floaty cotton voile looks great in front of French doors and dark silk Ikat surrounding a bed makes a striking alternative to headboards.

MATERIALS
For a door curtain to fit a door measuring 81in (206cm) × 36in (91.5cm)

Furnishing cotton for curtain front: 2½yd (2.3m) of 60in (150cm) fabric
Cotton ticking for lining: 2½yd (2.3m) of 60in (150cm) fabric
Wool flannel interlining: 3½yd (3.2m) of 45in (115cm) fabric
Herringbone webbing for joining interlining and for pleats: 1¾yd (1.6m) of 2in (5cm) webbing
Matching sewing thread
Curtain rings and rod to measure

For a braided tie-back measuring 23½in (60cm) long
Furnishing cotton for tie-back: ½yd (46cm) of 60in (150cm) fabric
Cotton ticking for tie-back: ¼yd (23cm) of 60in (150cm) fabric
Kapok stuffing: 8oz (225g)

The Fabrics
Heavy, close-woven furnishing cotton in a glowing kilim design of cinnabar red, slate blue, stone, black, and white contrasts harmoniously with striped cotton ticking.

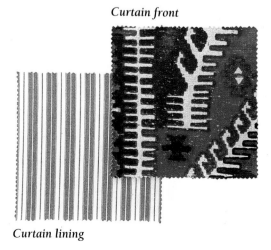

Curtain front

Curtain lining

Making the Curtain

1 *To join flannel interlining, cut a length of webbing to the curtain width (here 59in [150cm] plus 1in [2.5cm] for seam allowances). Place 1 piece of flannel along center of tape and zigzag stitch together. Match second piece of flannel against first piece and stitch down onto tape in same way.*

2 *Spread flannel out flat and, having cut front fabric, lay it on top, right side up. Smooth out creases starting from center and pin the 2 layers together at 8in (20cm) intervals, working outwards from the center in top to bottom rows.*

3 *Cut away any surplus flannel interlining at the edges of the front fabric.*

4 *Stitch a quilting line from top to bottom down center of curtain, using the pattern to keep straight. Repeat at no more than 8in (20cm) intervals to the left and right, finishing with a line ½in (1.25cm) from each edge. Use matching thread.*

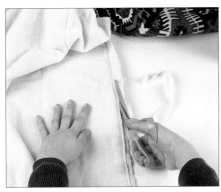

5 *Cut flannel back as close as possible to quilting line at each outer edge so that the side seams will be less bulky.*

6 *Cut lining fabric to same length but 1in (2.5cm) narrower than front fabric and pin together along long sides, right sides together. Stitch down long sides ½in (1.25cm) in from edge, leaving about 8in (20cm) unstitched at hem end of seam for adjusting curtain length.*

7 *Pin front and lining fabrics together at top, starting in the center and working out toward both sides. The front fabric will form an edge ¼in (6mm) wide on both sides of lining fabric. Stitch along top ½in (1.25cm) from edge.*

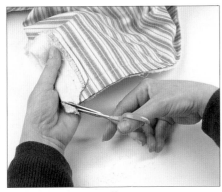

8 *Cut away seam allowance at corners to reduce bulk and give a sharper corner when curtain is turned right side out. Turn curtain right side out.*

9 *Using a tape measure, pin equidistant pleats at top (see p. 14 for pleating techniques). We inserted 5 pleats, each 2in (5cm) wide.*

10 *For hanging the curtain, cut 7 8in (20cm) strips of webbing. Fold them in half and pin against the pleats' inside edge and to the curtain back at each end. Make top of loops level with curtain top.*

11 *Starting 1¼in (3cm) from top of the curtain, stitch a rectangle with crossed diagonal lines to anchor pleat and webbing together. You are stitching through all thicknesses so you should use a strong needle.*

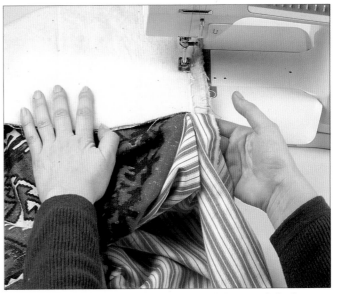

12 *Hang curtain by hooking rings through loops and check length. Pin up sides of front fabric hem accordingly, right sides together, and stitch up both sides ½in (1.25cm) from edge.*

Making the Curtain (cont.)

13 *Cut away corner, turn right side out and pin up hem of front fabric. Sew up by hand with a herringbone stitch (see p. 11) ⅜in (1cm) in from raw edge.*

14 *Pin up lining fabric hem allowance, right sides together, and stitch up both sides ½in (1.25cm) from edge. Cut away corner and turn right side out.*

15 *Pin lining to outer fabric along unstitched sides and bottom and slipstitch together (see p. 11). Hang the curtain.*

Making a Braided Tie-back

To make the tie-back, first estimate the necessary finished length by looping a measuring tape around the curtain drawn back as you like it (see page 9 for measuring techniques). Add 6in (15cm) to this length for the shortening effect of the batting and braiding. Cut two strips of curtain fabric and one of lining fabric to this length, all 8in (20cm) wide.

Fold each strip right sides together along the longer edge and stitch with a ⅜in (1cm) seam allowance to form narrow tubes. Press the seams open and turn tubes right side out. Positioning seams at center back, stitch across one edge of each tube, ½in (1.25cm) from edge. Fill each with kapok – aim for a soft, even filling.

When tubes are full, stitch across the other ends, ½in (1.25cm) from edge to prevent the kapok from escaping. Stitch the three tubes flat together at one end, making sure the long seams are hidden underneath, and braid them together loosely. Stitch the other ends of the tubes flat together and stitch rings to each end to attach the tie-back to the wall.

Variations

Sumptuous Silks

A dark silk Ikat lined with glowing silk checks would make a beautiful bedhanging. Crisp white bed linen and lace would contrast beautifully with its rich dark colors and you could tie it together by making an eiderdown from matching silks.

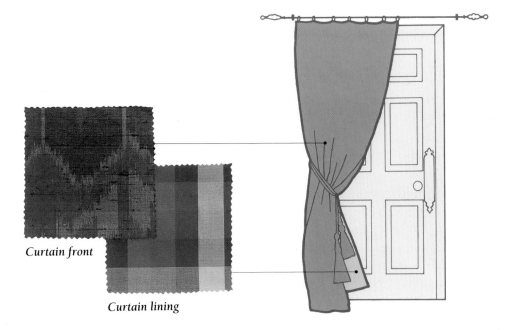

Curtain front

Curtain lining

Stripes and Stars

Floaty cotton voile looks stunning hung in front of French doors. Use the bright transparent stripes on the inside and the tiny gold stars on cream facing the outside. The combination conjures up bright, warm climates, and would look perfect with whitewashed walls, scrubbed wood, and sun streaming in.

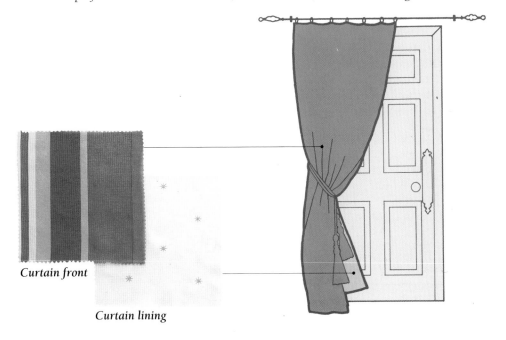

Curtain front

Curtain lining

Pleated Cupboard Curtains

*Rows of tiny cloud-gray stars on soft white cotton chambray
have been pleated to make cupboard curtains that epitomize
the fresh, unpretentious spirit of French country style.*

HOWEVER PRACTICAL, the modern fitted kitchen often lacks character. This can be remedied by borrowing from the traditional French country kitchen, which combined function and charm. Here, dishes, pantry items, and the like were stored in capacious *armoires de cuisines*. Pretty fabric curtains added color and hid clutter.

You can use the same technique to enliven your own kitchen. There is something particularly attractive about the contrast between the solidity of wooden furniture and the softness of fabric, and lining cupboard doors like this is an easy way to achieve it. The delicate folds in the fabric set off the hard lines of the furniture and the pleating also makes the cotton chambray less transparent.

You can achieve a similar effect more quickly by doing away with pleats and making a flat curtain or gathered

curtains from patterned fabric (such as those shown on page 79). The idea does not have to be confined to the kitchen. Bathrooms and bedrooms can also benefit from a delicate touch of texture and color. You can hang them using spring rods or plastic coated wire (see page 9 for techniques on hanging cupboard curtains) cut to the right length.

You can use sheers or lace, gathered or stretched flat, for the same light, airy look shown here. Darker, solid fabric matched to the paint color or harmonizing with natural wood would look handsome in a more formal setting. These fixed curtains have other applications too: sheer drapes can be used on French doors to let in light while preserving privacy and any suitable fabric can be attached to hinged wooden frames to make a room divider screen.

MATERIALS
All curtains to fit a cupboard with two windows measuring 12in (30cm) × 34in (86cm)

For two pleated curtains:
Cotton muslin for curtains: 2¼yd (2m) of 45in (115cm) fabric
White sewing thread
Curtain hardware (see p. 9)

For two flat curtains:
Close-weave cotton for curtains: 1¼yd (1.15m) of 45in (115cm) fabric
Matching sewing thread
Curtain hardware (see p. 9)

For two gathered curtains:
Cotton voile for curtains: 2 ¼yd (2m) of 45in (115cm) fabric
White sewing thread
Curtain hardware (see p. 9)

For two pleated and tufted curtains:
Cotton muslin for curtains: 2¼yd (2m) of 45in (115cm) fabric
Silk embroidery yarn
White sewing thread
Curtain hardware (see p. 9)

The Fabric
*Subdued gray-blue stars subtly
dot delicate white cotton voile.*

Curtain

Making Pleated Curtains

1 Measure and cut a piece of fabric 2¾in (7cm) longer than the height of the cupboard opening and 3 times the width. Pleat and pin it (see p. 14 for pleating techniques) at regular intervals straight onto an ironing board cover (here we make ½in [1.25cm] wide pleats).

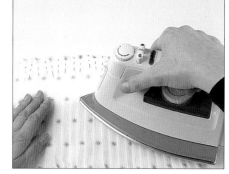

2 Having pulled the pleats straight and ensured both ends are even, press the pleats in position.

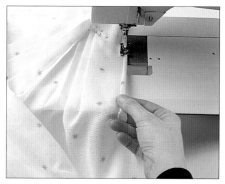

3 Check that the pleated curtain is at least 2in (5cm) wider than the cupboard and stitch a ¼in (6mm) wide hem down each side. Stitch at both ends to keep the pleats in place.

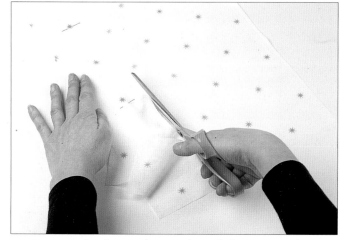

4 To secure the pleats and create channels for curtain rods, cut 2 strips of fabric 3½in (9cm) wide and 2in (5cm) longer than the width of the cupboard opening. Before cutting, use pins to ensure that the design is in the same position on each strip.

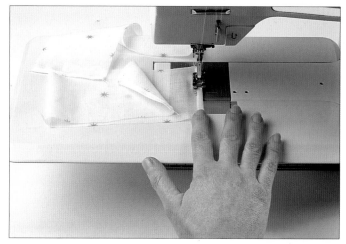

5 Make a ¼in (6mm) hem at the ends of each strip. The strips should now be the same length as the width of the pleated curtains.

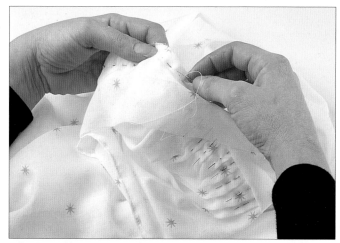

6 Pin and baste a strip along the top of the curtain right sides together (the hems of the strip should be facing outwards), making sure the pleats remain flat.

7 Stitch the pleated curtain to the strip from the back of the curtain with a ⅜in (1cm) seam allowance, and remove the pins and basting.

8 *Zigzag stitch along the seam edge from the front to prevent the open weave material from ravelling.*

9 *Turn and pin the strip onto the wrong side of the curtain tucking under a ⅜in (1cm) hem. Stitch carefully along the hem and repeat the process from step 6 for attaching second strip to bottom of curtain. Repeat entire process for second curtain. See p. 9 for techniques on hanging cupboard curtains.*

Curtain Styles

The simplest cupboard curtain of all (near right) exploits a beautiful, medium weight cotton which is just stretched over the cupboard opening. Cut a piece of fabric to the depth of the opening plus 5in (12.5cm) for hems and channels for rods, and the width of the opening plus 2in (5cm) for side hems.

Another alternative is voile, here printed with mulberry red heraldic animals. It gathers beautifully into a translucent curtain which hints at the cupboard's contents while concealing the clutter. To achieve the gathering effect shown here, you need a piece of fabric 3 times wider than the cupboard opening, plus the normal allowances for sides and for seams. In place of voile, you could use other delicate fabrics such as lace or net, which would both be particularly suitable in a bedroom.

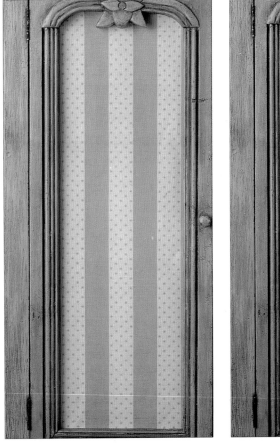

Making a Tufted Curtain

You can pull together a tricky color scheme by customizing your fabric with matching tufts. Here we have used silk embroidery yarn, but you could also use fine satin ribbons tied into tiny bows on a more open weave fabric, giving the curtain a feminine look, or shells, beads, or pearls for textural interest.

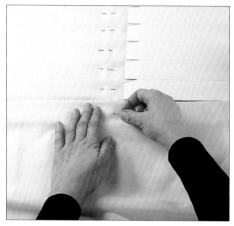

1 *Using a sheet of cardboard at least the width of the cupboard opening as a template, mark it with parallel lines 2in (5cm) apart. Cut out a triangle at the end of each line as shown and use it as a guide for pinning and stitching the pleats (see p. 14 for pleating techniques and step 1 on p. 78).*

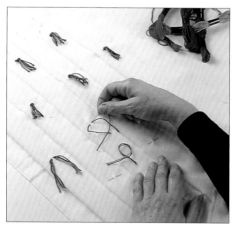

2 *Using a ruler for accuracy, mark where you want the tassels to go. Here we have created a diamond pattern by inserting them on alternate pleats in rows across. Cut equal lengths of the yarn and then thread them through from the front, one color at a time as shown. Check that protruding strands are equal in length and knot them together. Follow steps 2–9 of Making Pleated Curtains (pp 78–79) to finish off.*

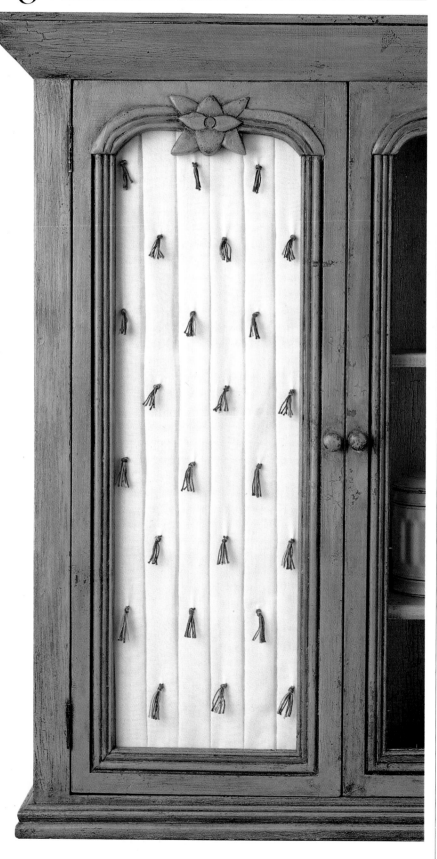

Variations

Blue Spots

Regular spots on slightly uneven woven cotton voile would look pretty gathered and used in a painted or polished wood country cupboard.

Curtain

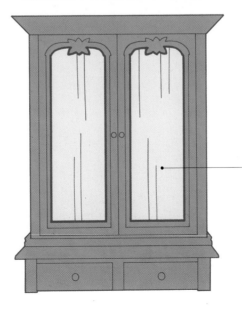

Pink Flowers

Nosegays of pink flowers on cotton muslin would suit a feminine bedroom. Use them for matching dressing-table skirts or swags.

Curtain

Gold Lions

Winged lions among the stars printed on cotton voile would look splendid gathered or pleated in a dining-room sideboard cupboard, hiding shelves of white crockery.

Curtain

Seating

Bench Cushion

Colonial Pillows

Patchwork Wool Pillow

Striped Satin Pillow

Woolen Throw

Bench Cushion

A color combination of crisp denim blue, red, and white stripes tied with bright red tape brings a welcome touch of comfort to a spartan seat.

A SOLID RECTANGULAR CUSHION (known as a squab cushion) serves a multitude of purposes. It can transform a blanket box or trunk into an ottoman, make a window seat into a cozy retreat, add comfort to garden furniture or a piano bench, or transform an antique fireside settle like this into inviting seating.

Our cushion covers exploit the harmonious partnership of coordinating, close-woven, denim-weight cottons. The cover-inside-a-cover is distinctive and simple to make. The bright red of the bows picks up the thin red stripe in the fabric used for the inside cushion and adds a welcome dash of color. We have reinforced the

link between the cushion and the two complementary pillows by using the same red for their piping.

The use of denim-weight cottons gives the cushion a casual air, but you can easily alter this. Tapestry fabric in soft, restrained colors, with matching plain silk for the inside cushion and accompanying pillows, would be lovely for a window seat in a grand living room. Or use a bright colored print of sunflowers in washable cotton to bring a bench cushion in your kitchen to life.

Here, we have made two medium-sized pillows out of matching fabrics to complement the bench cushion. You can vary their size, number, and shape according to the space available and your taste.

MATERIALS

For a bench cushion 13in (33cm) × 37in (94cm) × 2⅜in (6cm)

Striped denim for outer cushion: 1⅓yd (1.2m) of 45in (115cm) fabric
Striped denim for inner cushion: 1⅓yd (1.2m) of 45in (115cm) fabric
Cotton tape for ties: 2¾yd (2.5m) of 1in (2.5cm) tape
Red and navy blue thread
Zipper: 1yd (90cm)
Foam rubber cushion pad: 37in (94cm) × 13in (33cm) × 2⅜in (6cm)

For 2 accompanying pillows 16½in (42cm) square

Striped denim for pillows: 20in (50cm) of 45in (115cm) fabric for each pillow
Cotton tape for piping: 4½yd (4m) of 1in (2.5cm) tape
Piping cord: 4½yd (4m)
Matching sewing thread
Two feather-filled pillow pads: 16½in (42cm) square

The Fabrics

Indigo blue and wine red on a natural cotton ground, here spiced up with the scarlet red of the bows, is an association of colors that never fails in a combination of different stripes.

Pillow

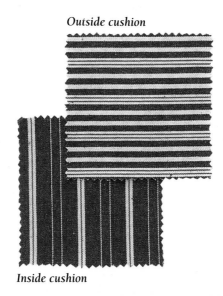

Outside cushion

Inside cushion

Pillow

Cushion bow and piping for pillows

Making the Cushion

1 *For the outer cover, measure and cut out fabric to required size. To do this, fold fabric in half lengthwise to width of cushion and add 4in (10cm) for seam allowances plus the cushion pad depth. To determine fabric length, add ¾in (2cm) for seam allowances plus twice the cushion pad depth to the required length.*

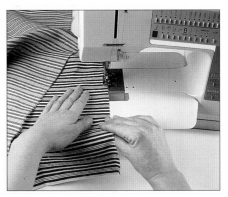

2 *Zigzag stitch along all the raw edges to prevent the fabric from ravelling.*

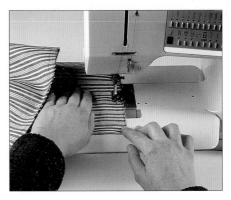

3 *Fold fabric in half lengthwise, right sides facing, and stitch along side seams, with ⅜in (1cm) seam allowance. Press seams open.*

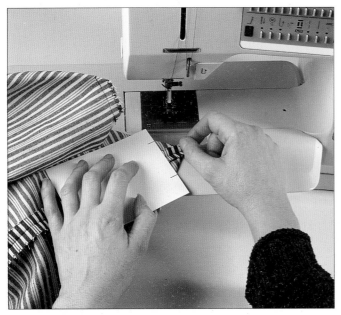

4 *Mark a piece of cardboard to match the cushion depth and place it diagonally across the opened-out corners. Stitch across the corners to create a box shape and trim corners to reduce bulk.*

5 *Turn in 2in (5cm) for hem of front opening. Pin in position and stitch all the way around.*

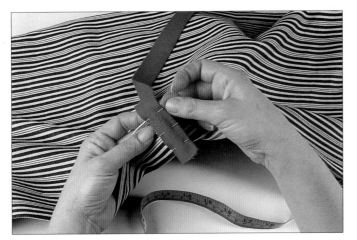

6 To make ties, cut 4 pieces of tape to desired length (here each is 21in [53cm] outside the cushion plus 2in [5cm] inside). Pin 2 pieces to hem of one side of cushion (here, pieces are 11in [28cm] in from seam on both sides). Pin other 2 pieces to hem in matching positions on the other side of the cushion.

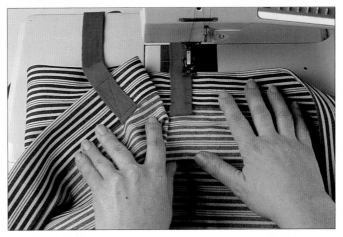

7 Attach tapes by stitching a rectangle and crossing inside it diagonally for added strength. Hem other end of tape by hand to prevent ravelling.

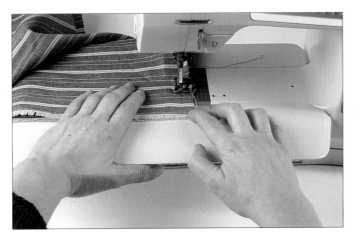

8 Cut out fabric for inner cushion. Fabric length is the same as outer cover, but, after folding in half lengthwise to width, add 1in (2.5cm) for seam allowances plus twice the depth of cushion pad. Zigzag stitch along all raw edges, fold fabric in half length-wise, right sides together, and stitch a seam 2½in (6.25cm) long at one end, with a ½in (1.25cm) seam allowance for zipper opening.

9 Press open seam and ½in (1.25cm) seam allowance for zipper. Starting at the stitched end, pin and baste open zipper in place on top of pressed seam allowance.

10 Turn the fabric right side out and stitch the zipper in place along both edges, using the zipper foot. Make sure pressed edges meet exactly. Turn wrong side out and stitch remaining seam allowance at other end of zipper. Press open seam.

11 Lay cover down so back seam with zipper is centered and then pin, stitch, and press open the 2 end seams, with ⅜in (1cm) seam allowance. Ensure that the zipper is partially open so the cover can be turned right side out after stitching. Remove basting stitches along zipper, turn right side out, and insert pillow pad.

Making Complementary Pillows

Both of these pillows are made in exactly the same way. For each cushion, cut a piece of fabric 17½in (44.5cm) square and two pieces 13in (33.5cm) × 17½in (44.5cm). Make sure that the stripes on the second two pieces go the same way and that each has a 17½in (44.5cm) side cut along a selvage if possible. Turn each selvage inside and stitch a ¾in (2cm) hem.

Lay the two rectangles on top of one another with the hemmed edges towards the middle and the right side of one facing the wrong side of the other. Adjust their position until between them they form a 17½in (44.5cm) square (they should overlap by approximately 7in [18cm], forming a flap for the pillow opening). Pin and stitch these pieces in position.

Make 70in (180cm) of piping for each pillow by stitching the red binding around the piping cord using a zipper foot (see page 14 for piping techniques).

Place front of pillow on top of back, right sides facing, and check that the stripes match and are going in the same direction. Pin and baste front and back together with piping sandwiched in the middle (see below). Clip piping corners to assist turning. Stitch around edge and zigzag along all raw edges to prevent ravelling. Turn right side out and press.

Repeat entire process for second pillow and insert pillow pads.

Variations

Antique Tapestry

A medieval flower design in soft tapestry colors would make an inviting window seat. Plain silks for the inside cushion and accompanying pillows pull out colors from the design. You could also make accompanying curtains in the same color or fabric.

Pillow

Outside cushion

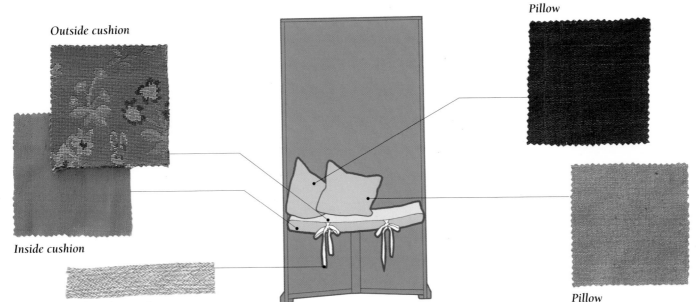

Inside cushion

Pillow

Cushion bow and piping for pillows

Pillow

Country Kitchen

Bold sunflowers on washable cotton perfectly color-matched with a tiny farmyard print makes a whimsical combination for a bench cushion in a bustling kitchen. Green ties bring out the green in both prints, and green is echoed again in piping around pillows of red and yellow.

Pillow

Outside cushion

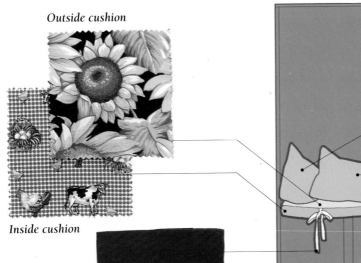

Inside cushion

Cushion bow and piping for pillows

Pillow

Colonial Pillows

A seductive nest of pillows piled into a wicker chair, in variations on a red and white theme. A simple lace insertion is accompanied by traditional American embroidery, Flying Geese patchwork, and the plainest of piecing.

A N EASY WAY to bring warmth to a room is with an inviting pile of pillows. They add color, interest, and comfort for minimal cost and effort. Pillow covers are quick and fun to make and give an instant lift to a room at a fraction of the cost of new upholstery and decoration. Be creative. You can mix and match color, pattern, and texture, and experiment with different trimmings.

This simple interior with its painted walls, wide plank flooring, and roomy chair is brought to life by accents of crisp red and white, picking up the red in the antique Boston rag rug. A collection of different fabrics and designs, linked by color, provides richness and variety. Checks, stripes, patchwork, and embroidery combine harmoniously together.

In the center pillow, the heavy white linen works well in partnership with the delicate cotton insertion lace. Both are set off by the solid red of the lining – a color combination used to equally good effect in the embroidery. The red and white gingham stripes in the flying geese patchwork pillow link it to the other two pillows. One has checks bordered by stripes; the other is backed by stripes.

Visible closures such as the bows shown here are a decorative alternative to conventional closures such as zippers or snaps.

Of course, when choosing colors you can use a wider palette. Try mixing primary colors, coordinating tapestry colors, or varying shades of a single color. Pillows are the perfect way to use up leftover scraps, or you can shop for interesting remnants.

Look for unusual trimmings. Braid and tassels can transform an ordinary cushion into something exotic and sumptuous. As for other decorations such as appliqué, embroidery, or stenciled motifs, the only limit is your imagination.

Lace Insertion Pillow

MATERIALS
*For a lace insertion pillow
16in (41cm) square*

Linen for pillow cover: ½yd
(46cm) of 45in (115cm) fabric
Cotton insertion lace: 1⅓yd
(1.22m) of 2¼in (5.7cm) lace
Cotton for pillow lining: ½yd
(46cm) of 45in (115cm) fabric
Matching sewing thread
Two ¾in (2cm) white buttons
Feather-filled pillow pad: 16in
(41cm) square

The Fabrics
A cheerful combination of red and white in a classic strip contrast of heavy white linen and delicate insertion lace, set off nicely by the strong red of the lining.

Pillow lining

Pillow cover

Pillow insertion lace

COMPONENTS

Below are the elements needed for a 16in (41cm) square pillow

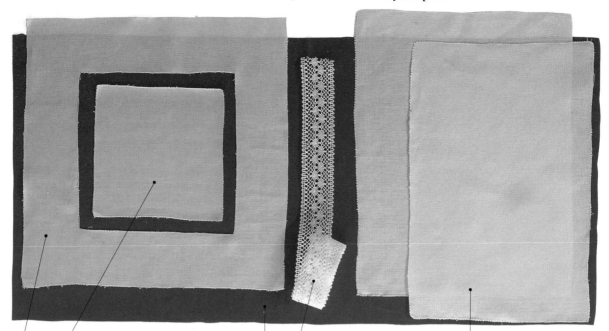

Pillow cover front center: 7½in (19cm) square (to be trimmed to fit exactly later)

Pillow cover front border: 16¾in (43cm) square with a 8¾in (22cm) square cut out of its center leaving an even 4in (10cm) border.

Pillow insertion lace: 2¼in (5.7cm) wide × 1¼yd (1.1m)

Pillow lining: 16¾in (43cm) × 36¾in (94cm)

Pillow cover back: one piece 10½in (27cm) × 16¾in (43cm); one piece 13in (33cm) × 16¾in (43cm)

Making the Pillow

1 *Having cut out the fabric for the pillow following the components photograph, zigzag stitch around all raw edges to prevent fraying. Press a ¼in (6mm) seam allowance around inside of the back of the border, cutting at corners to make it lie flat.*

2 *Turn border over to right side and, starting at a corner, pin lace around inside of border, just overlapping the seam allowance. Fold over the lace on the back side at corners as shown. Stitch from back following the pins, taking care not to catch the folded lace at the corners.*

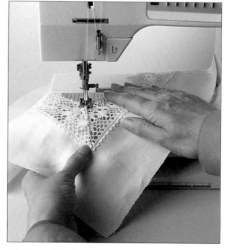

3 *Turn border over and zigzag stitch twice (⅛in [3mm] apart) across the corners of the lace diagonally. Pull the threads to the back and knot.*

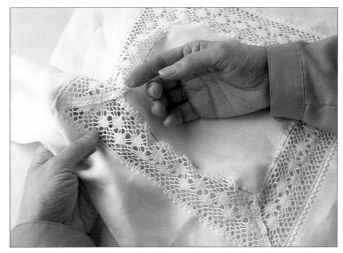

4 *Trim away surplus folded lace at the corners on the back, being careful not to cut through the stitching.*

5 *Trim center square to fit, allowing for a ¼in (6mm) seam. Press seam (cutting at corners) and pin center in position so lace just overlaps seam. Stitch close to selvage of lace.*

6 *For the cover back, stitch by hand or machine a 2in (5cm) hem along 1 longer side of both the back pieces. If the side is a selvage you need not turn the fabric under.*

7 *Pin the two back pieces so that the hems overlap and then pin cover front to back, right sides together. Stitch front and back together and zigzag ¼in (6mm) in from raw edges. Turn right side out and press. For directions on making buttonholes and sewing buttons see pp. 14 and 29.*

8 *To make lining pillow, cut out fabric following components photograph and stitch a ⅜in (1cm) hem at both ends. Fold over one end by 4in (10cm) and stitch up sides to make a pocket. Fold in half, right sides together, and pin and stitch a ⅜in (1cm) seam down both sides. Turn right side out and insert pillow pad, closing by pulling pocket flap over, like a sandwich bag.*

Variation

Medieval Bestiary

A forest green lining adds richness to a quaintly charming cotton print of animal woodcuts in soft green, brown, and cream. The simple cotton insertion lace adds to the general air of antiquity.

Pillow cover

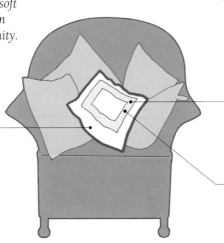

Pillow lining

Pillow insertion lace

Embroidered Good Morning Pillow

To make the pillow, cut out the fabric following the measurements below. Use dressmaker's carbon paper to transfer the embroidery template on page 19 to the center of the front cover and stem stitch (see page 11) the design. Stitch a 2in (5cm) hem, with ⅜in (1cm) turned under, on one of the longer sides of both back pieces. Pin the two back pieces with the hemmed edges towards the middle and adjust their position until between them they form a 16½in (42cm) square (they should overlap by approximately 3½in [9cm]). Pin front to back, right sides together. Stitch, with ⅝in (1.5cm) seam allowance, and trim corners. Turn right side out, press, and stitch all around 1in (2.5cm) from outer edge.

MATERIALS
Homespun cotton for cover: ½yd (46cm) of 45in (115cm) fabric
Matching sewing thread
Standard embroidery thread
Dressmaker's carbon paper for transferring template (see page 19)
Button: ¾in (2cm)
Feather-filled pillow pad: 13⅜in (34cm) square

Pillow front: 16½in (42cm) square

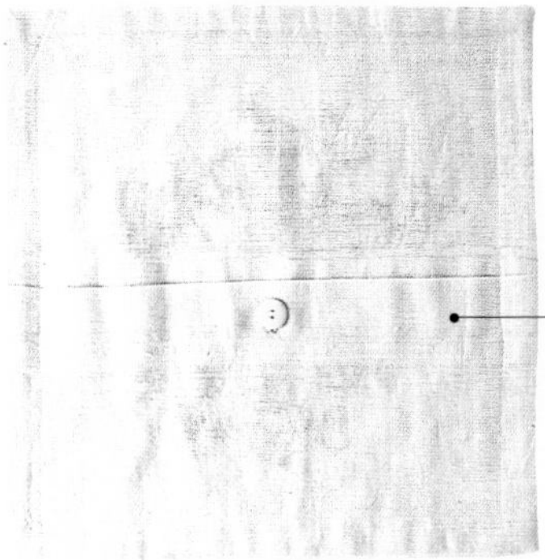

Pillow back: one piece 16½in (42cm) × 12½in (31cm); one piece 16½in (42cm) × 11¼in (28.5cm)

Flying Geese Pillow

To make the pillow, cut out the fabric following the measurements below (see page 10 for multiple cutting techniques). Stitch small triangles to large triangles to make 21 rectangles and stitch them together to make three strips of seven (see directions for *Making the Flying Geese Quilt*, steps 1–5 on page 39 for technique). Pin and stitch flying geese strips to 4 shorter front divider strips, right sides together and with a ⅜in (1cm) seam allowance. This should be done in such a way that the flying geese strips and divider strips alternate, with a divider strip on either edge. Stitch on the two longer divider strips top and bottom, right sides together and with a ⅜in (1cm) seam allowance, and press all seams open. For the pillow back, make a ¾in (2cm) hem on the longer edge of both pieces. Fold 2 strips for ties in half, wrong sides together, turn in seams and stitch to make ties. Stitch one tie to the center of the hemmed edge of the larger back piece. Stitch the other tie in the center of the other back piece, 3⅛in (8cm) in from the hem. Pin the back pieces so that they overlap in the middle, matching the size of the front, and pin to the front, right sides facing. Stitch front to back with a ⅜in (1cm) seam allowance and turn right side out. Press and insert pillow pad.

MATERIALS
Checked cotton for pillow back and pillow front divider strips: ½ yd (46cm) of 45in (115cm) fabric.
Large triangles for pillow front: ½yd (45cm) of 45in (115cm) fabric in total
Small triangles: ½yd (45cm) of 45in (115cm) fabric
Matching sewing thread
Feather-filled pillow pad: 15¾in (40cm) square

Pillow front divider strips: four strips, each 2⅛in (5.5cm) × 15⅜in (39cm); two strips, each 2⅛in (5.5cm) × 16⅞in (43cm)

Pillow front large triangles: 21 right-angled triangles in 3 coordinating patterns (see template on p. 15)

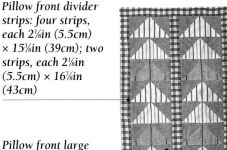

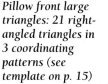

Pillow front small triangles: 42 right-angled triangles (see template on p. 15)

Pillow back: one strip 16½in (42cm) × 9½in (24cm); one strip 16½in (42cm) × 11½in (29cm)

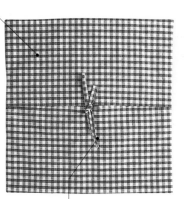

Pillow back ties: two strips, each 1¼in (3cm) × 11¾in (30cm)

Red Mitered Pillow

To make the pillow, mark and cut out fabric following the measurements given. Cut diagonal edges and pin, stitch, and press the pillow front borders in same way as with *Provençal Tablecloth* (page 112, steps 2–3), but attach pieces right sides together instead of wrong sides together. Attach the center panel as with *Provençal Tablecloth* (page 113, steps 4–6) but again attach pieces right sides together instead of wrong sides together. For the pillow back, make a ¼in (6mm) hem along 1 long side of both strips. Fold loop strips in half, wrong sides together, and stitch with a narrow turning. Fold these in half to make loops and stitch them to the back of one of the hems, spacing them evenly. Pin back strips together with a 3⅛in (8cm) overlap and pin to cover front, right sides together. Stitch around edges with a ⅜in (1cm) seam allowance. Turn right side out and sew on buttons (see page 14). Press and insert pad.

MATERIALS
Wide checked gingham for front: ⅓yd (30cm) of 45in (115cm) fabric
Striped cotton for front and back: ½yd (46cm) of 45in (115cm) fabric
Matching sewing thread
Two ¾in (2cm) buttons
Feather-filled pillow pad: 15¾in (40cm) square

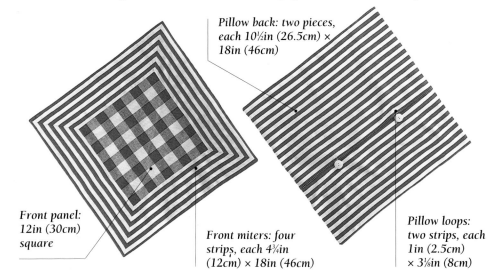

Pillow back: two pieces, each 10½in (26.5cm) × 18in (46cm)

Front panel: 12in (30cm) square

Front miters: four strips, each 4¾in (12cm) × 18in (46cm)

Pillow loops: two strips, each 1in (2.5cm) × 3⅛in (8cm)

Bow-Tied Gingham and Stripes Pillow

To make the pillow, cut out the fabric following the measurements given. Fold ties in half widthwise, wrong sides together, and stitch to make ties, folding under raw edges (see page 14 for techniques on making ties). Make a ⅜in (1cm) hem along one of the shorter sides of the pillow front and sew front cover ties to outside of hem, spacing them equidistant from each other and the pillow front edges. Turn over hemmed edge by 2¾in (7cm), wrong sides together. Stitch up sides, making a pocket. Sew pillow back ties in corresponding positions on pillow back as those on pillow front, 2¾in (7cm) from selvage. Pin front to back, right sides together (with ties and facing on outside), and stitch around edges with a ⅜in (1cm) seam allowance. Fold over opening seam allowance corners 45° and stitch to neaten. Turn right side out and press.

MATERIALS
Gingham for front and ties: ½yd (46cm) of 45in (115cm) fabric
Striped cotton for back and ties: ½yd (46cm) of 45in (115cm) fabric
Matching sewing thread
Feather cushion pad: 15¾in (40cm) square

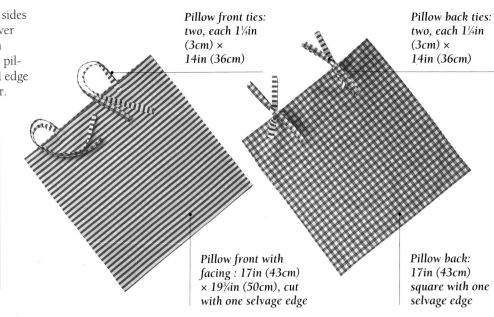

Pillow front ties: two, each 1¼in (3cm) × 14in (36cm)

Pillow back ties: two, each 1¼in (3cm) × 14in (36cm)

Pillow front with facing : 17in (43cm) × 19¾in (50cm), cut with one selvage edge

Pillow back: 17in (43cm) square with one selvage edge

Patchwork Wool Pillow

*A textured tweed pillow with a shaggy fringe offers a soft
haven of warmth and comfort perfect for a winter evening
spent in a leather armchair by the fireplace.*

WINTER DICTATES a radical rethinking of furnishings and fabrics. Floral linen, cotton checks, and tiny prints in bright colors should give way to warm wools and tweeds when the evenings lengthen and there is a chill in the air.

As the fabric changes, so should the colors. The warm chestnut and russets of bare bark and fall leaves offer instant comfort.

Before you start, make sure your pillow form is in good condition. Throw out any that have lost their shape and substance and invest in new ones. Down or feathers fill a pillow more luxuriously than synthetic fibers, which soon become lumpy or stiff. Always measure

fabric against forms carefully so that your finished cover fits snugly. Underfilled pillows seem old and tired.

The pillow shown here is simple to make: patches of subtly colored Harris tweed alternating with a bold cream and brown check, accentuated by the deep beige fringe and the corduroy backing.

The dark, subdued colors were chosen to fit in with the rich browns of the table and chair, and the plaid squares match the checked wallpaper.

Use the rich, earthy colors of Guatemalan woven cotton to provide a brighter look or, if you want to retain the warm texture of wool, you could use two contrasting shades of corduroy or plain velvet.

MATERIALS
For a pillow 22in (56cm) square

Harris tweed for front squares:
⅓yd (30cm) of 45in (115cm)
fabric
Checked tweed for front squares:
¼yd (23cm) of 45in (115cm)
fabric
Fine-wale corduroy for back: ⅔yd
(61cm) of 45in (115cm) fabric
Natural cotton rug fringing for
fringe: 2½yd (2.25m)
Zipper: 20in (51cm)
Matching sewing thread
Feather-filled pillow pad: 22in
(56cm) square

The Fabrics
*A checkerboard of classic wool – peat brown Harris
tweed enlivened with a hint of unexpected green and
fox red, contrasting with a bold cream and brown
check discreetly etched with blue.*

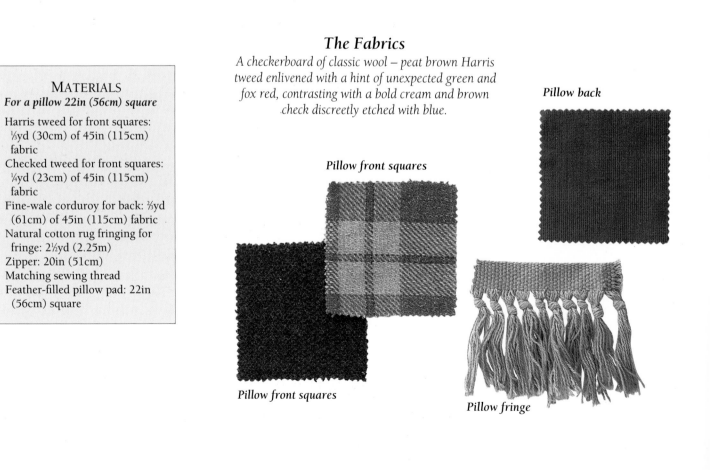

Pillow back

Pillow front squares

Pillow front squares

Pillow fringe

COMPONENTS

Below are the elements needed for a 22in (56cm) square pillow

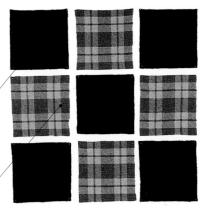

Harris tweed pillow front squares: 5 squares, each 8½in (21.5cm) square

Checked tweed pillow front squares: 4 squares, each 8½in (21.5cm) square

Pillow back: 2 pieces, each 12in (30.5cm) × 23in (58.5cm)

Pillow fringe: 2½ yd (2.25m)

Making the Pillow

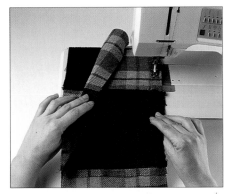

1 *Using the components photograph as a guide for size and pattern, cut, pin, and stitch the front squares right sides together into three strips, with a ½in (1.25cm) seam allowance (see p. 10 for multiple cutting techniques).*

2 *Press seams open from wrong side, using a damp cloth to protect the wool.*

3 *Again using the components photograph as a pattern guide, pin and stitch 2 strips right sides together, with a ½in (1.25cm) seam allowance. Check pattern is correct and attach third strip in same way. Press seams as before.*

4 *Starting in the center of one edge, baste a continuous piece of fringe to pillow front, right sides together, with the fringe's seam pointing outwards. Match ends of fringe edging together and overstitch as shown above.*

5 *Slash fringe edging at the corners so that edging will lie flat when stitched.*

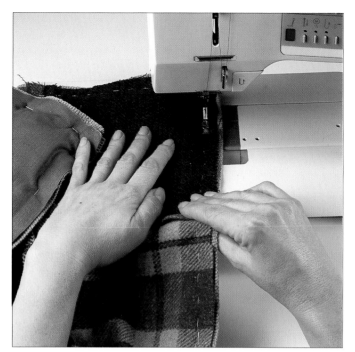

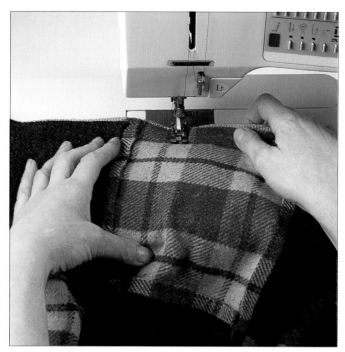

6 Having cut pieces for pillow back following components photograph and inserted zipper following instructions for Striped Satin Pillow (steps 1–2, p. 102), pin back and front right sides together. Using zipper foot, stitch around pillow through all layers with a ½in (1.25cm) seam allowance.

7 Overstitch ends of fringe edging within seam allowance to strengthen it and prevent ravelling. Turn right side out and insert pillow pad.

Variation

Autumn Colors

Guatemalan woven cotton in rich, earthy colors paired with coarse cotton in bright pumpkin make a cheerful checkerboard. The piping is natural herringbone braid and the back is close-woven cotton with tan and conifer green stripes.

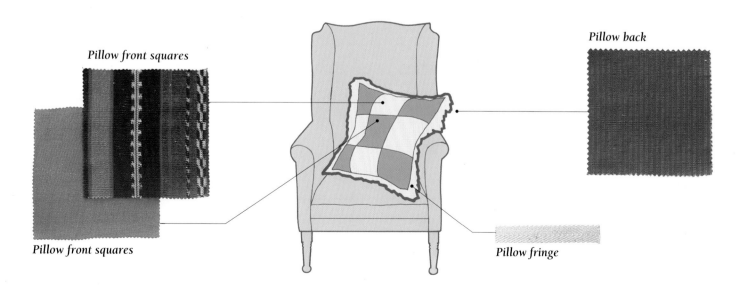

Pillow back

Pillow front squares

Pillow front squares

Pillow fringe

Striped Satin Pillow

A simple shape given exotic treatment in sumptuous satins.
Braid and tassels, the crisp definition of black piping, and a
burgundy and black version of the fabric for the back produce
a mood of Far Eastern opulence.

ONE OF THE PLEASURES of soft furnishings is that they do not have to be expensive or even permanent. Pillows are the furnishing equivalent of jewelry – the perfect way to emphasize and accent a color scheme. Pillows can be made to match mood or season: this extravagant combination of fabrics and colors is perfect for a boldly theatrical interior and quick to make besides. A single pillow looks good, and a pile of them in slightly different weaves and shades would be spectacular.

Striped woven satin, finished with braid and tassels, creates an exotic Far Eastern effect. The broad lines of black braid isolate the bright stripes of the center panel from the more delicate stripes of the border fabric. The braid also accentuates the striped design and, together

with the black piping around the edge, gives the pillow its geometric definition.

While your budget may not allow the use of costly fabrics on a large scale, pillows such as this one provide an opportunity to use velvet, brocade, or silk left over from dressmaking or bought as remnants. Antique textiles such as small tapestry panels, or a piece of needlepoint you have stitched but do not know how to display, can similarly be shown off to advantage.

You can also use this design to create a more unassuming look. Try raw silk in a combination of wide stripes of cream and caramel brown, with matching braid in place of the black. Or, use fabrics that are more easily cleaned such as cotton and linen, and choose colors that would look at home on your kitchen bench.

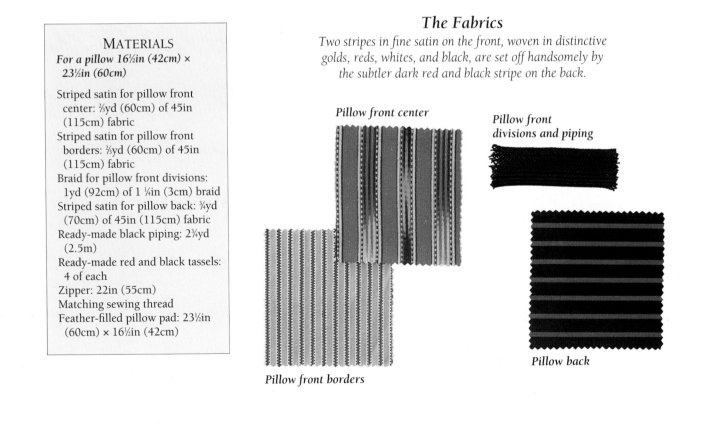

MATERIALS
For a pillow 16½in (42cm) ×
23½in (60cm)

Striped satin for pillow front
  center: ⅔yd (60cm) of 45in
  (115cm) fabric
Striped satin for pillow front
  borders: ⅔yd (60cm) of 45in
  (115cm) fabric
Braid for pillow front divisions:
  1yd (92cm) of 1 ¼in (3cm) braid
Striped satin for pillow back: ¾yd
  (70cm) of 45in (115cm) fabric
Ready-made black piping: 2¾yd
  (2.5m)
Ready-made red and black tassels:
  4 of each
Zipper: 22in (55cm)
Matching sewing thread
Feather-filled pillow pad: 23½in
  (60cm) × 16½in (42cm)

The Fabrics
Two stripes in fine satin on the front, woven in distinctive
golds, reds, whites, and black, are set off handsomely by
the subtler dark red and black stripe on the back.

Pillow front center

Pillow front
divisions and piping

Pillow back

Pillow front borders

COMPONENTS

Below are the elements needed for a 23½in (60cm) × 16½in (42cm) pillow

Pillow front borders:
2 pieces, each 6½in
(16.5cm) wide, 17¼in
(44cm) long

Pillow front center:
12¾in (33cm) wide,
17¼in (44cm) long

Pillow back: 2 pieces, each 9⅛in
(23.25cm) wide, 24¼in (62cm) long

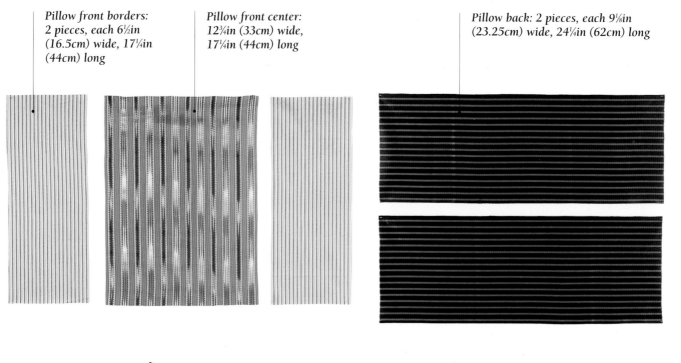

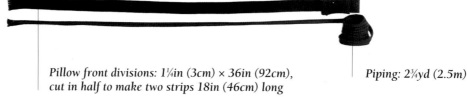

Pillow front divisions: 1¼in (3cm) × 36in (92cm),
cut in half to make two strips 18in (46cm) long

Piping: 2¾yd (2.5m)

Making the Pillow

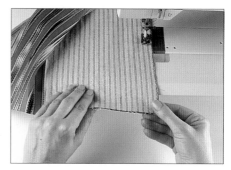

1 Cut out fabric following components photograph and pin 2 back pieces right sides together along long edge. Place the zipper next to the edge, equidistant from either end, and pin. Stitch a ½in (1.25cm) seam from each end to the zipper, overstitching inner end of seams strongly. Open out wrong side up and press open small seams and ½in (1.25cm) seam allowance for zipper (see p. 14 for zipper techniques).

2 Turn right side up and, holding the zipper in place at the back, pin it from the right side. Make sure pressed edges meet exactly. Using zipper foot, stitch around zipper in 1 stage.

3 Using components photograph as a guide, join the 3 pieces of fabric for front by pinning right sides together and stitching down the two seams, with ⅜in (1cm) seam allowances. Press seams open on wrong side.

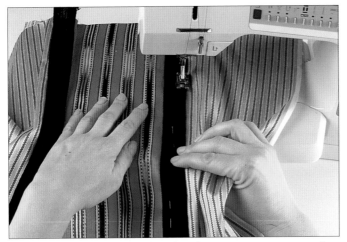

4 With fabric right side up, pin braid in position over center of seams (if braid is stretchy, baste instead of pinning), leaving a ⅜in (1cm) overhang at either end to be trimmed later. Stitch along edges of each piece of braid.

5 Leaving zipper partially open, pin front and back right sides together, with ready-made piping in between (see p. 14 for piping techniques), its seam allowance facing outwards. Leave 1in (2.5cm) piping spare at zipper seam. Starting at zipper seam, use zipper foot to stitch around edge of pillow with a ⅜in (1cm) seam allowance. Leave corners unstitched for insertion of tassels.

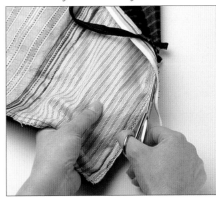

6 Turn the pillow right side out and pin the ends of tassels into the corners which have been left open. Be sure tassels are all the same length.

7 Turn the pillow wrong side out and sew in the tassels and the corners by hand, using double thread. Snip into the seam allowance of the piping cord at the corner so that piping lies flat when it is stitched.

8 Zigzag stitch around the edge of the seam to prevent ravelling and trim away any surplus fabric, braid, and piping cord. Turn pillow right side out and insert pillow pad.

Variation

Discreet Stripes

Raw silk in wide stripes of cream and caramel brown, divided by matching lightly flecked braid creates a cool, unfussy look.

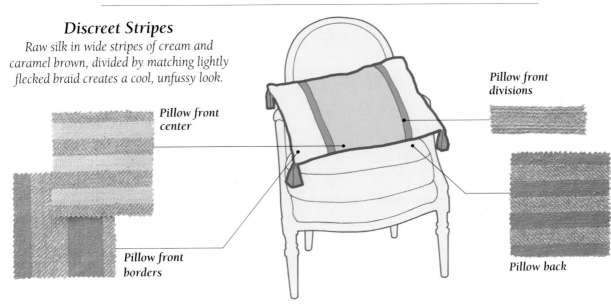

Pillow front center

Pillow front divisions

Pillow front borders

Pillow back

Woolen Throw

*An all-purpose blanket-cum-comforter, this luxurious,
warm woolen throw adds old-world style and elegance to the
plainest chair or sofa.*

A THROW IS A practical finishing touch to any room, pulling colors together. It provides warmth and comfort and can revitalize old, worn upholstery at low cost. It is highly adaptable and can be made large or small, for indoors or out, in a whole range of fabrics to suit your room and the season. Best of all, it is very easy to make.

Our throw is made in soft reversible wool bound in plaid tweed. The even plaid binding shown here gives a tidy, symmetrical effect. Binding fabric should be cut on the bias so that it will stretch and lie flat when stitched. Neatly mitered corners are also essential (see p. 12 for mitering techniques).

Here we have chosen rich, autumnal colors which complement the chair fabric, the Oriental rug, and the warm tones of natural wood, but the variations are infinite. Instead of reversible fabric, as used here, choose a patterned fabric, then select a solid color fabric that picks up the colors of the pattern for the back and the binding. Wool is an obvious choice because of its warmth and softness, so consider a heathery tweed finished with blanket stitching in thick woolen yarn. Or, a lovely woven wool can be fringed and knotted to give a finish to the edge.

A throw of Indian woven cotton or loose-weave linen is suitable for summer. It can double as a picnic blanket or make patio furniture and garden seats more inviting.

Texture is all-important: it must be soft to the touch and drape well. The throw is a sensuous item that should invite you to wrap yourself up in it or should drape casually over a chair or sofa for all to admire its rich colors and graceful folds.

The Fabrics

*Thick, soft wool in reversible camel and navy, bound
neatly in tobacco brown and navy plaid tweed,
enlivened by a subtle streak of cinnabar red.*

*Reversible fabric
for throw*

Throw binding

MATERIALS
*For a throw measuring
65in (165cm) × 72in (183cm)*

Reversible wool for throw: 2yd
(1.8m) of 80in (200cm) fabric
Checked wool for binding: 1¼yd
(1m) of 60in (150cm) fabric
Navy and camel sewing thread

Making the Throw

1 For the binding, cut out strips 5¼in (13.25cm) wide (see p. 13 for binding techniques). Join the strips together, matching tweed, so that you have 2 strips at least 70in (178cm) long and 2 at least 80in (200cm) long. Press joined seams flat, using a damp cloth to protect the wool.

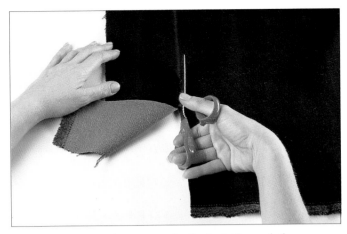

2 Using a carpenter's square and tailor's chalk, mark the reversible fabric to the size you want and cut along the chalk lines. Here we have made a rectangle measuring 65in (165cm) × 70in (178cm).

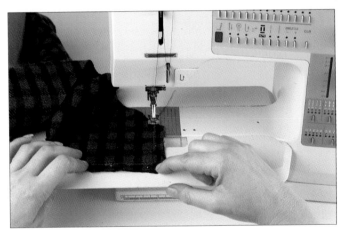

3 Pin and stitch binding along edges of one side of rectangle, leaving a few inches unstitched before each corner and enough binding to shape miter. Cut, pin, and sew miters in position as shown, leaving ½in (1.25cm) open at each end of miter seam and overstitching there (see p. 12 for mitering techniques).

4 Having pressed the miter seam open, pin the ½in (1.25cm) openings precisely at the corners and complete the stitching of the binding to the throw (see p. 12 for mitering techniques).

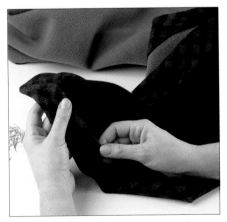

5 Turn right side out and press and pin under hem on unstitched edge of binding to meet stitched line.

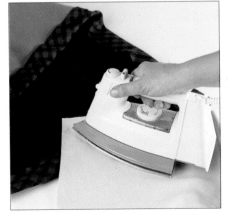

6 Press with a damp cloth, guiding the hem into place with your fingers as you go.

7 Slipstitch the reverse-side hem by hand and press again to eliminate pin marks.

Throw Edgings

Different edge finishes suit different fabrics: fray tapestry to reveal its rainbow warp; finish blanket wool with a classic blanket stitch (see p. 10); fray and knot coarse hand-woven silk tweed (see below).

1 *Remove crosswise threads one at a time to create 3in (7.5cm) of fringe.*

2 *Taking a ⅜in (1cm) section of fringe at a time, make a loose knot and tighten it down to the woven fabric.*

Variations

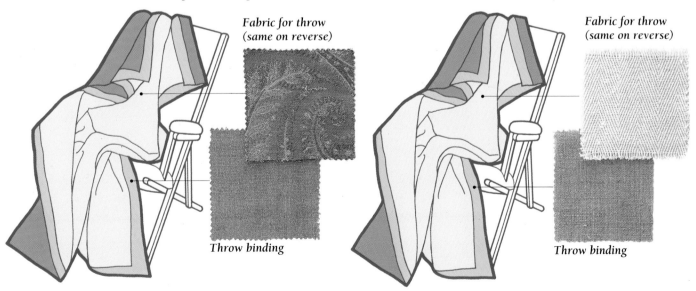

Subtle Paisley

Great swirls of blue paisley tapestry fabric in wool and cotton, bound with terracotta silk, make a sophisticated throw that would be at home in simple or richly patterned interiors.

Fabric for throw (same on reverse)

Throw binding

Summer Naturals

Heavy herringbone weave cream cotton from India bound with unbleached linen scrim, make the perfect summer throw to soften a garden bench or bring elegance to upholstered furniture.

Fabric for throw (same on reverse)

Throw binding

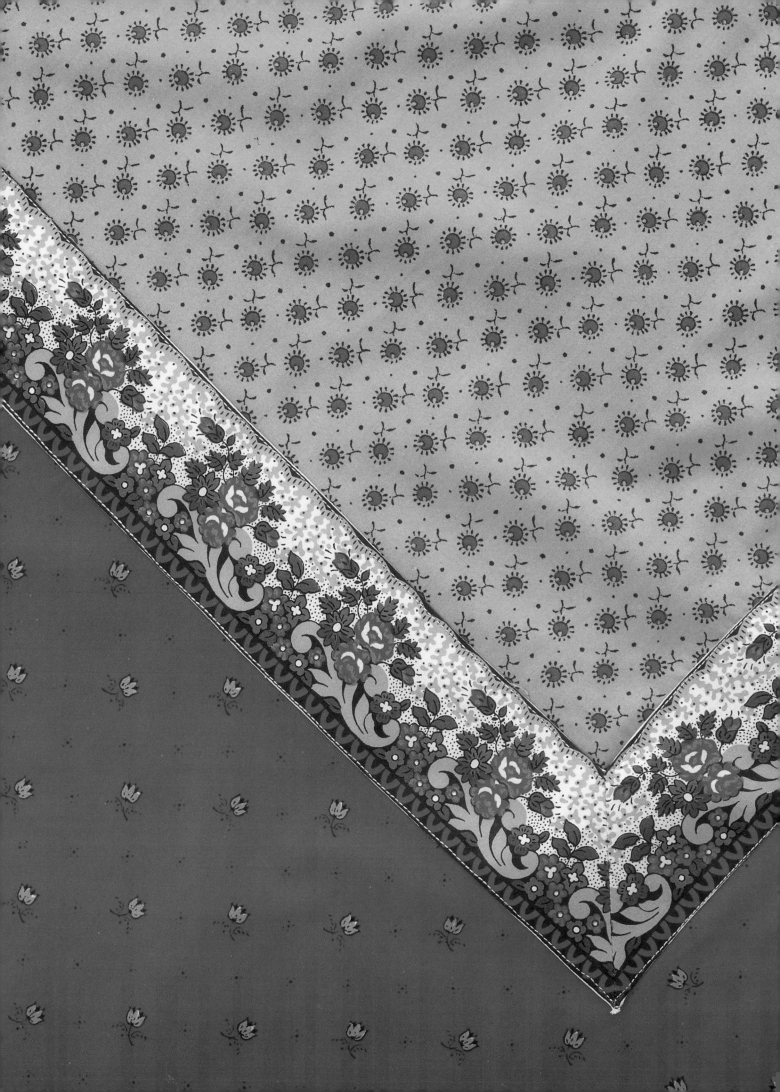

TABLECLOTHS AND BAGS

Provençal Table Linen

Quilted Tote Bag

Picnic Tablecloth and Bag

Provençal Table Linen

*A set of table linen brimming with Mediterranean
exuberance. Bold, bright colors and intricate patterns perfectly
evoke summer in the south of France.*

SOME FABRICS CAPTURE the essence of the culture that created them. This tablecloth, made of French Provençal cotton, is a glorious example.

The French took these delicate designs from Indian block printing and transformed them into brilliantly hued prints by borrowing the colors of the Mediterranean landscape. Provençal fabrics are now exported all over the world and interior designers have proven that their intricate designs and vibrant colors are at home in every environment.

The secret to using these fabrics is to exploit the range of harmonizing colors and patterns, matching up the contrasting elements and tying together the different variations of shade and pattern with one of the many border designs. The colors for the various components need not match exactly (in fact, a more lively effect comes from using related, but not matching colors), but they should come from the same color family.

Here, we have used two contrasting fabrics: brilliant yellow with a tiny red floral motif, and deep red with a small yellow flower. They are joined by a border fabric with red, blue, and yellow flowers on a white background. The colors of the flowers unify the yellow and red of the main fabrics, while the white background lightens the whole effect. The dark color of the underskirt acts as a foil to the brighter shades and busy pattern of the square overcloth.

If you prefer less contrast you can still use the same design. Create a subtler combination with colors such as cinnamon, reddish brown, and cerulean blue.

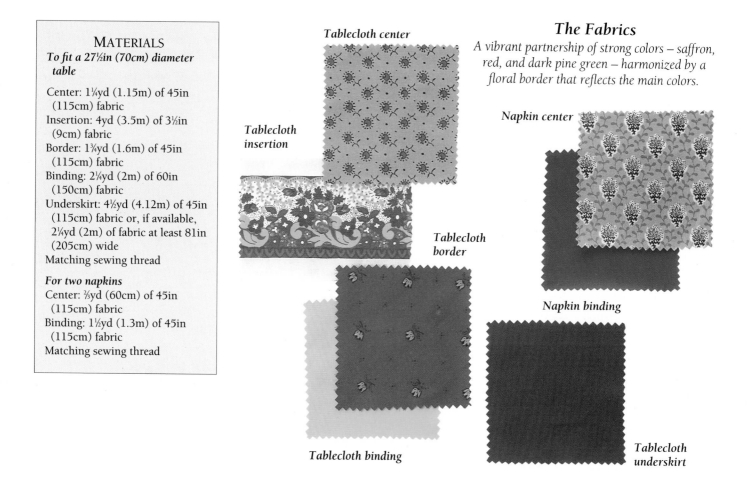

MATERIALS
To fit a 27½in (70cm) diameter table

Center: 1¼yd (1.15m) of 45in (115cm) fabric
Insertion: 4yd (3.5m) of 3½in (9cm) fabric
Border: 1¾yd (1.6m) of 45in (115cm) fabric
Binding: 2¼yd (2m) of 60in (150cm) fabric
Underskirt: 4½yd (4.12m) of 45in (115cm) fabric or, if available, 2¼yd (2m) of fabric at least 81in (205cm) wide
Matching sewing thread

For two napkins

Center: ⅔yd (60cm) of 45in (115cm) fabric
Binding: 1½yd (1.3m) of 45in (115cm) fabric
Matching sewing thread

Tablecloth center

Tablecloth insertion

The Fabrics
A vibrant partnership of strong colors – saffron, red, and dark pine green – harmonized by a floral border that reflects the main colors.

Napkin center

Tablecloth border

Napkin binding

Tablecloth binding

Tablecloth underskirt

COMPONENTS

Below are the elements needed for a 50in (127cm) square tablecloth

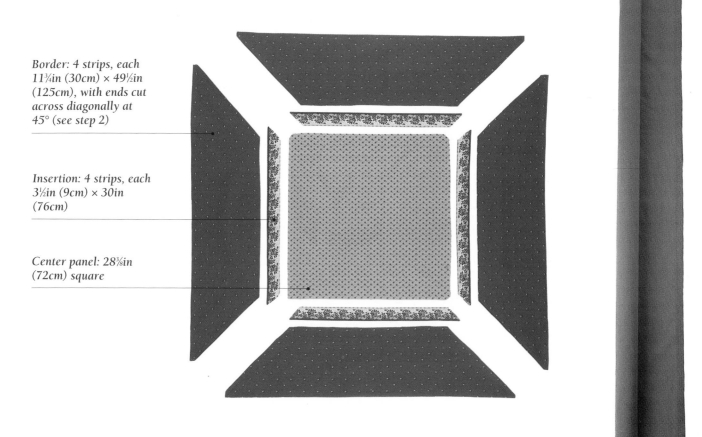

Border: 4 strips, each 11⅞in (30cm) × 49½in (125cm), with ends cut across diagonally at 45° (see step 2)

Insertion: 4 strips, each 3½in (9cm) × 30in (76cm)

Center panel: 28⅜in (72cm) square

Binding: 4 strips, each 2¼in (6cm) wide, at least 20in (51cm) long

Underskirt: 81in (205cm) square

Making the Tablecloth

1 Mark and cut the fabric for the insertion and border (see step 2 for cutting the border strips) using the components photograph as a guide and following the pattern, not the weave, of the fabric.

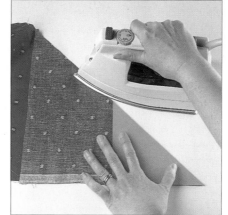

2 To make the diagonal ends on the borders, fold over and press the ends as above, using a 45° template as a guide. Place the shorter side of each border against a side of the center panel to check they are the same length and cut along the fold.

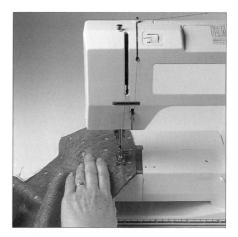

3 Pin and stitch the 4 border strips right sides together along the diagonal ends, with a ⅜in (1cm) seam allowance and stopping ⅜in (1cm) short of the inside corners (see p. 12 for mitering techniques). Draw thread through to back and knot.

4 *Place the border over the center panel fabric, aligning the patterns. Mark where they meet with tailor's chalk on the right side of the center panel, allowing for a ½in (1.25cm) seam allowance. Cut out center panel along marked lines.*

5 *Baste and stitch border to center panel wrong sides together, with a ½in (1.25cm) seam allowance. Leave the mitered corners open (see p. 12 for mitering techniques).*

6 *Press open the seam on the right side, trimming any surplus fabric at the corners.*

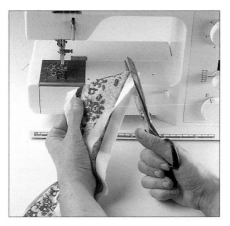

7 *Place insertion strips centrally over pressed seams. Mark, press, and cut miters (see p. 12 for mitering techniques), allowing for a ⅜in (1cm) seam at corners.*

8 *Press under seam allowances on both sides of insertion so they can be appliqued straight onto the tablecloth.*

9 *Stitch miters of insertion right sides together, leaving inside and outside seam allowances open. Draw thread through to back and knot. Trim outside corners of miter to reduce bulk.*

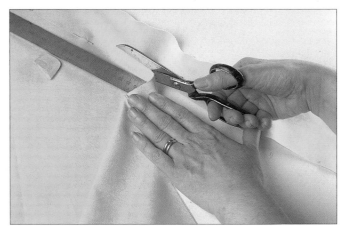

10 *Lay tablecloth on flat surface. Starting at corners, pin insertion centrally over pressed seams of border and center panel, following the pattern and matching up the miters. Stitch carefully, ⅛in (3mm) in, along the inside and outside edges of insertion.*

11 *Cut and join binding fabric (see p. 13 for binding techniques) to make 4 strips of binding, each 2¼in (6cm) wide, at least 50in (127cm) long. Press ⅜in (1cm) seam allowances on both sides.*

Making the Tablecloth (cont.)

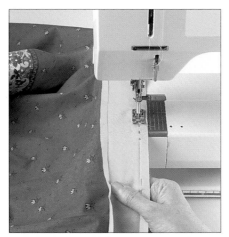

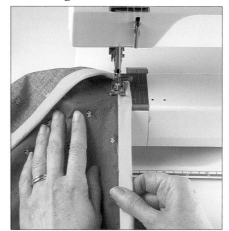

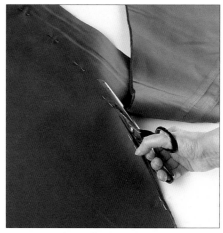

12 *Pin a strip of binding to the right side of 2 opposite border edges and stitch along pressed seam. Fold over and press, tucking under the other seam allowance and ensuring that the binding is at least ⅛in (3mm) wider on the underside.*

13 *Stitch in a "ditch" close to the seam on the top side of the binding, ensuring that you catch the underside of the binding easily. Repeat for other 2 border edges, turning under excess at corners and stitching by hand (see p. 13 for techniques on stitching corners). Press thoroughly.*

14 *For the underskirt, fold and press fabric in half twice and then fold it in half diagonally to form a triangle. Draw a segment of an arc using a pencil fastened to a tack with string (see p. 10 for techniques on cutting a circle). Pin around arc and cut through all layers of fabric. Open out and stitch a narrow hem all around.*

Making the Napkins

To make two napkins, mark and cut two 20in (51cm) squares of the center fabric, following the pattern, not the weave of the fabric. Cut and join binding fabric (see page 13 for binding techniques) to make 8 strips of binding, each at least 20½in (52cm) long, 2¼in (6cm) wide. Press ⅜in (1cm) seam allowances on both sides of each binding strip and attach binding to napkin following the instructions for attaching binding to the tablecloth above (steps 12–13).

Variations

Autumn Russets

Lively printed and plain cottons in bright terracottas and hyacinth blue combine to make a tablecloth and napkins ideal for the natural country look – white walls, seagrass matting, a log fire, and comfortable armchairs slipcovered in linen.

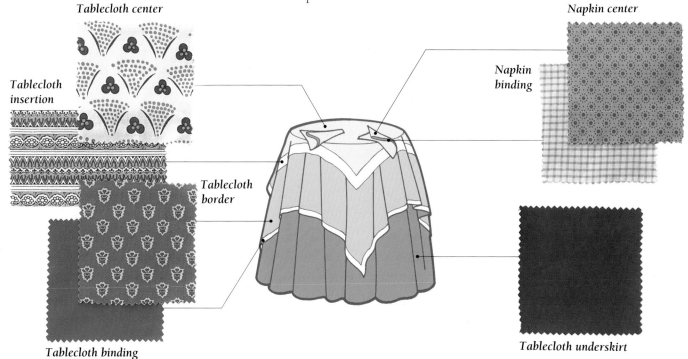

Tablecloth center

Tablecloth insertion

Tablecloth border

Tablecloth binding

Napkin center

Napkin binding

Tablecloth underskirt

Rainbow Linens

Fine linen dyed in strong, plain colors is combined here with an underskirt in Guatemalan stripes.

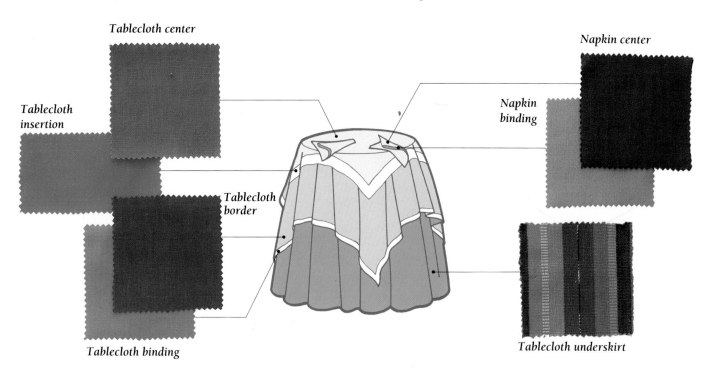

Tablecloth center

Tablecloth insertion

Tablecloth border

Tablecloth binding

Napkin center

Napkin binding

Tablecloth underskirt

Quilted Tote Bag

*Warm, muted sunshine colors in a trio of fabrics make
a handsome, all-purpose holdall for storing all kinds
of clutter.*

THIS HANDSOME TOTE BAG is perfect for holding all sorts of bits and pieces, like needlework in progress, and you will be able to make the bag, from cutting out to completion, in an afternoon. Once this simple solution has transformed your life, you will discover there are any number of uses for good looking, portable, washable totes. A big tote can store a spare duvet or sleeping bag; a little tote is perfect for diapers and baby accessories; a medium-sized tote will hold fabric scraps saved for that pieced quilt you are going to make one day.

Here we have used two different striped cottons for the outside of the bag and the lining, and a coordinating plaid for the base and binding. To give it a natural look, the bag is closed by thick, undyed cotton rope, threaded through metal eyelets, and finished with large twine tassels you can make yourself. The trio of fabrics combine for a warm, muted effect.

You could replace these with any number of different colored and patterned fabrics, harmonizing them with the room you will keep the bag in. Indeed, using the same construction principles, you can adapt the bag's shape and size to your own needs. It can even work as a travel or beach bag. In the latter case, you should use waterproof nylon or rubber for the lining and synthetic rope for the closure.

MATERIALS

*For a bag with a 39in (100cm)
circumference, 39in (100cm) deep*

Thick cotton for bag outside: 1¼yd
(1.15m) of 45in (115cm) fabric
Thick cotton for bag lining: 1¼yd
(1.15m) of 45in (115cm) fabric
Thick cotton for binding and base:
½yd (46cm) of 45in (115cm)
fabric
Lightweight batting: 1⅔yd (1.5m)
of 45in (115cm) fabric
Knitting cotton for tassels: 1 skein
Natural cotton rope: 3¼yd (3m)
Metal eyelets: 8
Matching sewing thread

The Fabrics

*Thick cotton in harmonizing stripes and plaid, in
shades of rich, golden yellow, soft smoky gray-blue,
dusty brick red, and bleached wood.*

Bag outside

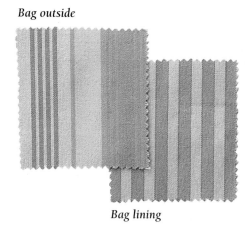

Bag lining

Bag binding and base

COMPONENTS

Below are the elements needed for a bag with a 39in (100cm)
circumference, 39in (100cm) deep

Bag outside: 40in
(102.5cm) × 39in
(100cm)

Bag lining: 40in
(102.5cm) × 39in
(100cm)

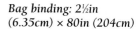

Bag binding: 2½in
(6.35cm) × 80in (204cm)

Rope for closure:
3¼yd (3m)

Knitting cotton for
tassels: 1 skein

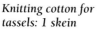

Bag base: 2 circles with a
radius of 7in (17.75cm)

Making the Bag

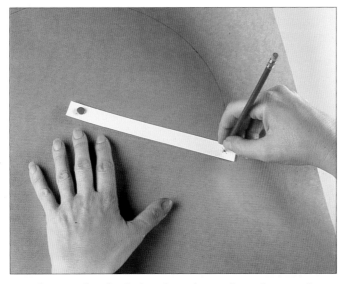

1 *Make a template for the base by tacking a sheet of paper at least 16in (40cm) square to a work table. Tack a narrow strip of cardboard 8in (20cm) long to the center of the paper and make a tiny hole at the other end of the card 7in (17.75cm) from the tack to insert pencil. Slowly spin pencil in strip to draw a circle. Cut it out.*

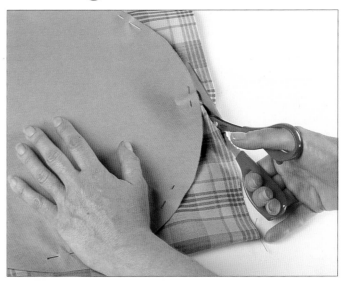

2 *For the base, pin the circle to a doubled piece of fabric to cut out 2 circles at once. If you are using a large plaid like the one shown, ensure that the circle is centered on the pattern.*

3 Use template to cut out batting to the same size as the circles and pin the 3 layers together with the batting in the middle. Stitch 2 evenly spaced quilting lines in both directions across base, making a square in the center.

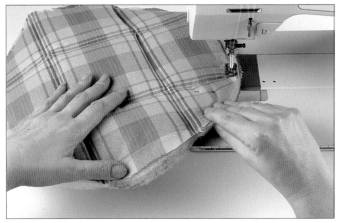

4 Stitch around edge of the base with ⅛in (3mm) seam allowance to keep layers together. Trim excess batting.

5 Cut out fabric for bag outside and lining following components photograph and cut a piece of batting to same size. Pin outside, batting, and lining together 2in (5cm) in from 1 edge from top to bottom. Work across fabric, pinning lines at 5in (13cm) intervals (for quilting lines) until you reach the far edge. Stitch lines from top to bottom.

6 Trim any excess batting from bag edges and zigzag stitch down raw edges on both sides of bag to neaten.

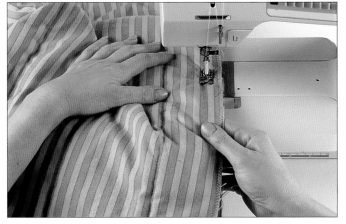

7 Fold bag in half, right sides together, and stitch to make a cylinder with a ½in (1.25cm) seam allowance.

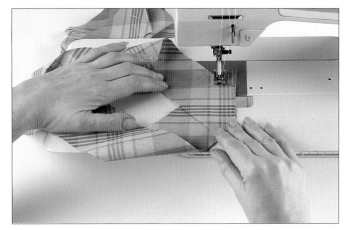

8 Cut and join binding to make 2 strips, each at least 40in (102cm) long, to edge top and base of bag (see p. 13 for binding techniques). If using plaid as here, be careful to match the plaid when stitching strips together.

Making the bag (cont.)

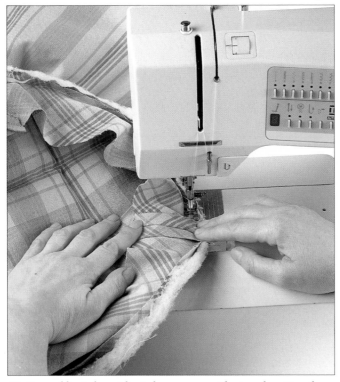

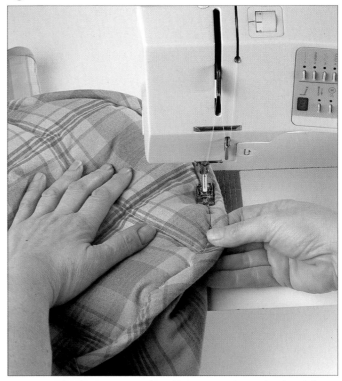

9 Pin and baste bag sides to base, wrong sides together. Turn bag right side out and pin and stitch 1 of the strips of bias binding to base, right sides together, with a ⅜in (1cm) seam allowance, joining bias ends together with a straight seam.

10 Turn binding over to sides of bag, pin under a ⅜in (1cm) hem, and press. Stitch in a "ditch" from the base of the bag through to the sides, catching the binding on the sides of the bag.

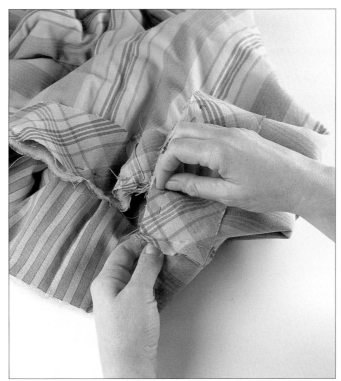

11 Pin and stitch other strip of bias binding to top of bag right sides together, with a ⅜in (1cm) seam allowance, joining bias ends together with a straight seam. Turn binding over to inside of bag, pin under hem, and press. Stitch in a "ditch" from the outside of the bag through to the inside, catching the binding all the way around on the inside as with the base in step 10.

12 Hammer eyelets in position at equal intervals around the bag top, following the instructions on the package. Here 8 eyelets were used, positioned at approximately 4in (10cm) intervals, all 5½in (14cm) from the bag top. Remember that you need an even number of eyelets so that when you lace the rope through, both ends will finish up on the outside.

Making the Tassels

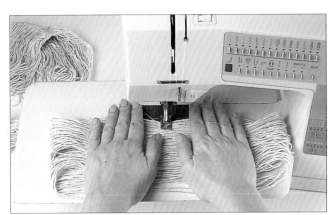

1 To make string tassels, wind the knitting cotton 80 times around a piece of cardboard, 20in (50cm) wide.

2 Carefully slide the string from around the piece of cardboard and stitch across the middle of the hank, using a long stitch setting. Cut the loops at either end as evenly as possible.

3 Hold the stitching line of the hank around the length of rope and stitch in position by hand with a darning needle. Wrap more string around to strengthen the join and stitch over and over until the tassel is secure.

4 Flip string over to cover rope end and wind more string tightly around the tassel. Stitch through it to hold firmly in place and trim the tassel. Thread the other end of the rope through the eyelets so that both ends are outside the bag. Trim the rope to the desired length and make and attach a second tassel following the steps above.

Variation

Blue Heraldic

This mythical beast, frolicking among stylized flowers on cerulean cotton, would look handsome lined with striped cotton in coffee and cream. The small blue check stands out crisply as the binding and base, and the tassels are in matching colors.

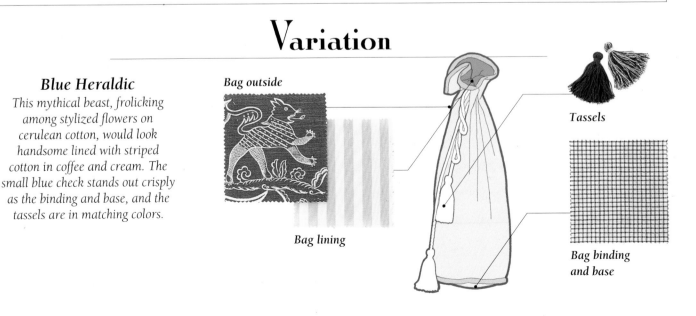

Bag outside

Tassels

Bag lining

Bag binding and base

Picnic Tablecloth and Bag

Civilized equipment to make your picnics stylish and comfortable: a summery tablecloth or blanket, and a bag to carry it and other picnic essentials.

SUMMER IS THE SEASON for relaxed, impromptu picnics. When the mood strikes, you will want to be up and out with the minimum of fuss. Our bag and tablecloth-cum-blanket will be at the ready for just such occasions.

The tablecloth is made from a ripe cotton print backed by rubberized silk to make it waterproof. Other options are thin rubber or plastic-coated cotton – less luxurious but more durable than silk. Manmade fibers (such as the nylon used for waterproof clothing) are also suitable. For the outer fabric, choose any tightly woven furnishing grade cotton that is easy to launder. Checks, stripes, and floral patterns all offer an informal summery look.

Cotton corduroy is a good choice for a heavier-duty rug. Whatever you choose, the tablecloth will only take an hour or so to make and will become an indispensible

accessory to outdoor living. You can use it to cover garden tables and seats at home as well as on outings.

The bag, which is also lined with rubberized silk to make it waterproof, should prove equally indispensible. It's perfect for stuffing with the tablecloth, a book, and something to eat and drink, and simply slinging it over your shoulder. Its long handles, securely stitched for added strength, have been specially designed with this in mind, and its pocket, large enough to hold a thermos, bottle, or cutlery neatly solves the problem of transporting all those awkward odds and ends essential for the perfect picnic.

This tablecloth and bag are made from the same fabric, but you could use different fabrics for each, even mixing solid, stripes, pattern, and check so long as the colors work well together.

MATERIALS
For a tablecloth 47in (120cm) × 59in (148cm)

Furnishing cotton for front: 1⅓yd (1.22m) of 60in (150cm) fabric
Rubberized silk for backing: 1⅓yd (1.22m) of 60in (150cm) fabric
Matching sewing thread
Tissue paper

For a bag 15in (38cm) wide × 18in (46cm) deep
Furnishing cotton for bag outside and pocket: ⅔yd (61cm) of 60in (150cm) fabric
Rubberized silk for lining: ½yd (46cm) of 60in (150cm) fabric
Herringbone webbing for handles: 4½yd (4m) of 1in (2.5cm) webbing
Matching sewing thread
Tissue paper

The Fabrics
A ripe collection of "summer fruit" colors in a rich furnishing cotton, backed with celadon green rubberized silk. The bag is lined with the silk and has strong natural herringbone webbing handles.

Tablecloth backing and bag lining

Tablecloth front and bag outside

Bag handles

COMPONENTS

Below are the elements needed for a 47in (120cm) × 59in (148cm) tablecloth and a 15in (38cm) × 18in (46cm) bag

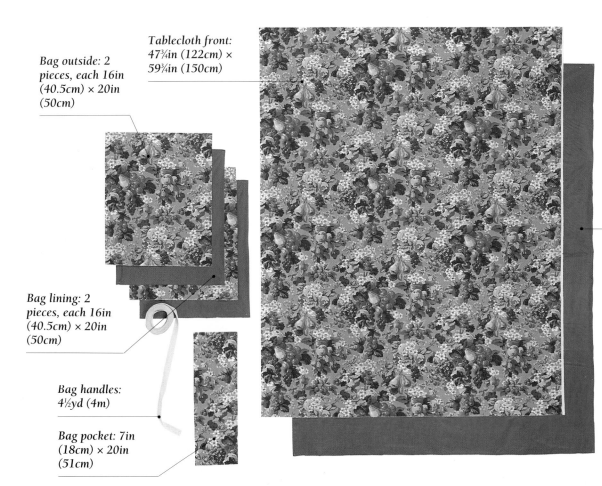

Bag outside: 2 pieces, each 16in (40.5cm) × 20in (50cm)

Tablecloth front: 47¾in (122cm) × 59¼in (150cm)

Tablecloth backing: 47¾in (122cm) × 59¼in (150cm)

Bag lining: 2 pieces, each 16in (40.5cm) × 20in (50cm)

Bag handles: 4½yd (4m)

Bag pocket: 7in (18cm) × 20in (51cm)

Making the Tablecloth

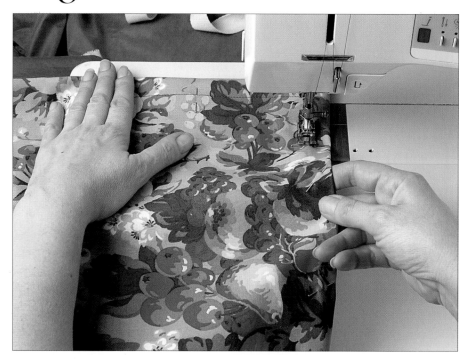

1 *Mark and cut out front and backing following components photograph. Pin front and backing right sides together. Stitch along all 4 sides with a ⅜in (1cm) seam allowance, leaving a 12in (30cm) gap on one side to turn cloth right side out. If rubber sticks to the feed-plate of the machine, stitch through tissue paper.*

2 *Trim corners to reduce bulk and turn cloth right side out. Hand stitch the opening and overstitch the cloth using machine, 1in (2.5cm) from the edge, with thread to match underside.*

Making the Bag

1 *Mark and cut out fabric for bag following components photograph. Fold fabric for pocket in half, right sides together, and stitch across short side, with a ½in (1.25cm) seam allowance.*

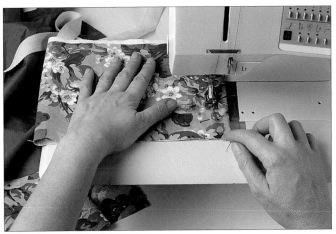

2 *Turn pocket right side out and topstitch pocket across the top, 1in (2.5cm) from edge, with matching thread.*

3 *Pin pocket so it is centered on piece of fabric that will be bag front and stitch along bottom of pocket 1in (2.5cm) from edge with matching thread.*

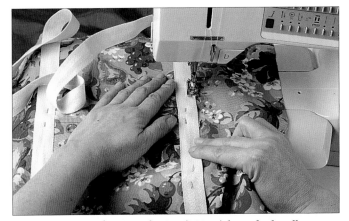

4 *Cut 2 pieces of tape, each 79in (200cm) long, for handles. Using sides of pocket as your guide, pin tape from base of bag front to top, covering pocket sides. Stitch 1 side of tape in place, turning across tape 1in (2.5cm) from bag top to leave seam allowance for attaching lining. Stitch down other edge of tape and attach.*

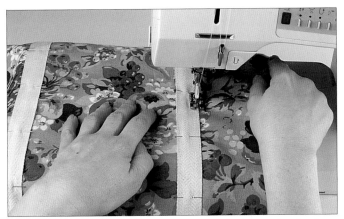

5 *Pin and stitch in same way to attach handle loop to bag back, measuring to make sure handles are in the same position as on the front.*

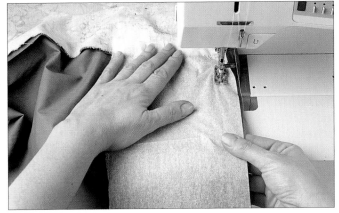

6 *With right sides together, pin and sew bag front to lining piece at top with ½in (1.25cm) seam allowance, taking care not to catch handles. Attach second lining piece to bag back in same manner. Matching top seams, stitch bag and lining front and backs right sides together with ½in (1.25cm) seam allowance sewing through tissue paper if rubber sticks.*

Making the bag (cont.)

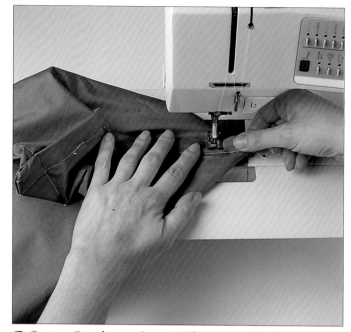

7 *Press side seams open with a cool iron. Turn right side out and topstitch all around top opening and handles 1in (2.5cm) away from edge to neaten.*

8 *Create a French seam (see p. 12) by sewing a ¼in (6mm) seam across the base of the bag on the outside, taking in both fabric and lining. Turn bag inside out and sew a ½in (1.25cm) seam along inside of base. Sew across corners to give the bag a rectangular base and trim corner fabric. Turn right side out.*

Variation

Reds and Greens

This mixture of solid, stripes, pattern, and checks are linked by their carefree summer garden colors and would combine well on cloth and picnic bag, with handles of bright red tape.

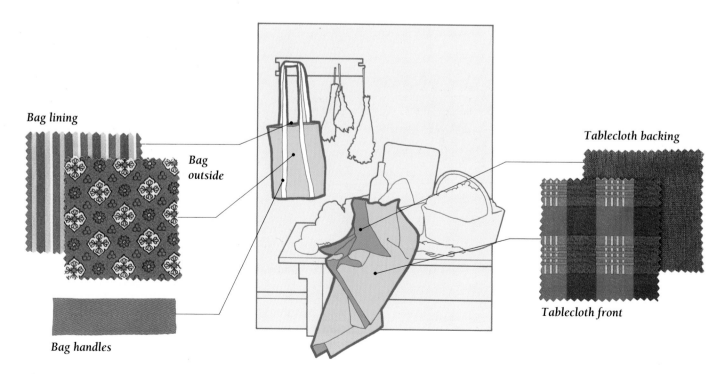

Bag lining

Bag outside

Bag handles

Tablecloth backing

Tablecloth front

Index